BEETHOVEN   A VICTORIAN TRIBUTE

# Beethoven
# A Victorian Tribute

BASED ON THE PAPERS OF SIR GEORGE SMART

by Percy M. Young

DENNIS DOBSON · LONDON

First published in Great Britain in 1976
by Dobson Books Ltd, 80 Kensington Church Street, London w8 4BZ

Printed in Great Britain by W & J Mackay Limited, Chatham

ISBN 0 234 77672 2

# Contents

# Plates

# Preface

Sir George Smart was the great architect of a British popular musical culture. He was the essential link in Britain between the classical and the romantic eras, the one acknowledged interpreter of the tradition of Handel (which was entrusted to him by those who had lived in Handel's time), the authoritative exponent of the works of Haydn, Mozart, and Beethoven, and the champion of the music of Mendelssohn and Spohr when that was new and unknown. Smart lived at a time when the duties of musical direction changed into the separate art of the conductor, and more than anyone in Britain he established the authority of this function. He was not only a good musician (albeit no composer), but also a meticulous administrator, a strict but understanding disciplinarian, and a mass of nervous and physical energy.

Smart may have had his base in London but he was a familiar figure throughout the land. His enthusiasm, skills, and integrity, endeared him to the thousands of modest music-makers who formed the choruses at the provincial festivals with which he was intimately connected. On this front Smart prepared the way for Henry Wood and Malcolm Sargent.

Sir George has always occupied a special place in English musical history on account of his knighthood. As in some other cases, Smart's knighthood was not earned for anything in particular and how fortuitous it was is shown in this book in the account of the circumstances that led to its bestowal. The lexicographers doubtless had good reason for allowing some facts of Smart's life to be published while others were suppressed. Why it should have been discreditable for him to have been a grocer is difficult to understand; but that fact certainly has been buried. By letting it out here (see p. 3) the supposition that the English were a nation of shop-keepers is strengthened.

Smart's private papers are an invaluable record not only of his own life but also of the development of musical taste and the spread of musical institutions during a long and significant period. Some part of his papers were published at the turn of the century. They were unfortunately so much bowdlerised, 'corrected', and generally and improperly maltreated that in their published form they had no value whatever.

The documents on which this present volume is based are the diary of Smart's visit to Bonn in 1845 as guest of the Beethoven Committee of that city, those other papers relating to his interest and connection with Beethoven, and the records of his general musical activities.

The 1845 Beethoven Festival marked the end of an era and the beginning of another. It finally made Beethoven 'classical', and determined that posterity would never presume to suggest anyone worthy of a higher place on Parnassus.

The pattern of events that led to this Festival, however, was part of a larger design, even if this was not appreciated by Sir George. Nonetheless, from what he wrote we notice that the scars of the Napoleonic Wars were still visible, that the idea of German unity was somewhat obsessive, and that the ugly shadow of anti-Semitism was only too evident. The visit to Bonn of Queen Victoria and Prince Albert, and of the King and Queen of Prussia, was diplomatically planned – to secure the continuing alliance of the British and the Germans and the support of the former for the long-term aspirations of the latter. All of this lies somewhere within Smart's narrative, and even more in the contemporary illustrations chosen to illuminate his text.

Smart gives us a tourist guide, an easy introduction to European diplomacy in the 1840's, and a musician's *vade mecum*. His account of his visit to Beethoven in 1825 has an authority of its own: the Beethoven he encountered was different from the character formulated by others. In his full account of the 1845 jamboree Smart steps out of period and describes an international gathering of musicians, or musicologists, or scholars of any kind, of any period. The story of the steamship excursion will do for today or for tomorrow.

Otherwise, however, Smart was very much a man of his own age (though long life enabled him to sample more than one age). When he travelled to Bonn in 1845 he went by ship and train, and his notes on the early hazards and pleasures of the railway age represent a nice and individual contribution to the literature of technology. It so happens that 1845 was particularly the year of the 'railway mania'. So it was described by *Punch* which gloomily saw industry being increasingly dominated by the machinations of George Hudson, the 'railway king', and the countryside polluted beyond redemption...The utilitarian Smart wondered whether bugles, as used on the Continental railways, might not be harnessed to the cause of safer transport (see p. 40). *Punch* satirically suggested at the same time that drums and trombones should be added to bugles to form standard equipment on the footplate.

Sir George enjoyed life. And in old age he retained his boyish sense of wonderment. In the broader sense he was no scholar, but his oddities of orthography and his naiveté of sentiment surround the solid body of his information with a rare degree of charm and sincerity.

What in this book is by Smart is as Smart left it except where his meaning is made clearer by editorial punctuation. It is distinguishable from the rest of the text by smaller type and indentation.

P. M. Y.

BEETHOVEN   A VICTORIAN TRIBUTE

# CHAPTER I

# Beethoven's English Advocate

In 1776 Mozart, a youth of 20, was living impatiently in Salzburg, where in July he composed the first of his works generally to be known – the Serenade in D major (K.250) for the wedding of Elisabeth Haffner. In Eisenstadt, Josef Haydn was lamenting two misfortunes; the destruction of his house by fire, and the rejection of his opera *La Vera Costanza* by the Court Theatre in Vienna which had commissioned it. In the Rhineland town of Bonn, the seat of the Archbishop-Elector of Cologne, the six-year old Ludwig van Beethoven was beginning to show progress in the piano and violin studies wished on him by his father. Interest in music in London in that year centred on the Italian opera at the King's Theatre and the concerts in Hanover Square organised by J. C. Bach and C. F. Abel.

On 10 May 1776, George Smart, a music-dealer and publisher in business at 331 Oxford Street, rejoiced that his wife had safely given birth to a son, whom he named George Thomas.

George Smart junior enjoyed a long life, which came to an end on 23 February 1867. That was the year in which Wagner completed *Die Meistersinger*, Brahms performed the newly written *Deutsches Requiem* in Vienna, and Paris heard Verdi's *Don Carlos* for the first time. The bright new star on the British horizon at that time was Arthur Sullivan, whose *In Memoriam* Overture had recently appeared and who went to Vienna in the autumn with George Grove in search of forgotten and mislaid masterpieces by Schubert.

The period covered by George Smart's life was one of the most decisive in European politics and music alike – containing in whole or in part the careers of Napoleon, Metternich, Bismarck, and Queen Victoria, on the one hand, and of Beethoven, Mendelssohn, Liszt, and Wagner, on the other. At one point the attention of crowned heads and politicians was briefly concentrated on one event in one town.

On 10 August 1845, Beethoven was officially registered on the roll of German national heroes, and his name added to the symbols representative of the ideal of political unity. On that day his monument was unveiled in Bonn. George Smart – who had been prominent in the cause of Beethoven's apotheosis – was not the least significant of those present on that occasion.

The Smarts originated in Wiltshire, where one Francis Smart – who died in 1791 at the age of 92 – maintained a clothier's business in Trowbridge throughout most of the eighteenth century. His son George (1745-1818), a keen music-lover, went into the music-selling trade in Bath, but finding opportunities for the enjoyment of music more limited than he liked, soon determined to try his luck in London. Here after working for James Bremner and William Napier, he established his own business. At the same time Smart took part in various musical enterprises in an active manner. At the Antient Concerts, for instance, he sang in the choir and also turned over the pages of the score for Joah Bates, a circumstance that was to have rather more significance than might have been thought at the time. In 1784 it is likely that he was the 'Mr Smart' named among the basses of the chorus of the Handel Commemoration. Two years after this event the New Musical Fund – a charitable organization established to relieve suffering in the profession – was established, and before long George Smart was acting as Treasurer.

Young George spent some part of his childhood at Ashford, Kent. As he had sustained a grave head injury in infancy it was thought better that he should be given a chance of restoring his health in the clean Kentish air. He went to a Mrs Pike's school, and while he was there Mr Fagg, a surgeon in Ashford, befriended him. Many years later he met Fagg's son, also a surgeon, in Hythe, as is related on p. 34.

It was, however, his father's intention that George should enjoy a better education than that provided by a dame school. He was, therefore, delighted when the boy was admitted to the Chapel Royal choir.

The Master at that time was Edmund Ayrton; the organists, Samuel Arnold – editor of the first considerable edition of Handel's works – and Thomas Dupuis. Young Smart was instructed by all three. Very soon after his admission he was one of the 'Ten Chapel Boys' who sang in the Handel Commemoration in Westminster Abbey. In the following years he became proficient on harpsichord, organ, and violin, in singing techniques, and in the theory of composition. At the same time he prudently acquired a working knowledge of business method and accountancy.

How true it was that England was a nation of shopkeepers is demonstrated by the career of George Smart who for half a century at least was one of the most influential musicians in England. He was also a qualified grocer.

On 1 July 1790, George Thomas Smart, 'son of George Smart, Music Seller', was apprenticed to William Impey, a member of the Grocers' Company who specialized in pharmacy. Having entered this trade, although still a member of the Chapel Royal choir, Smart thoroughly applied himself to its mysteries and on October 1 1797, he took up the Freedom of the Grocers' Company at Grocers' Hall in the City of London.[1]

Meanwhile Smart was beginning to establish himself as a musician. After leaving the Chapel Royal choir he was sometimes required to deputise at the organ for Arnold and Dupuis. The experience was useful – Arnold required him to play also at Westminster Abbey of which he was organist – but he received no fee. However, he was able to earn a stipend as organist of St James's Chapel, Hampstead Road, with which new foundation there were family connections. On 6 March 1794, the '1st Public Performance in London of Mr Smart Jun.' was advertised, his opportunity coming during a New Musical Fund concert at the King's Theatre, Haymarket. Advertised as a pupil of J. B. Cramer, he played a Concerto for the 'Grand Forte-Piano' by Dušek.

At this time Smart was becoming a regular member of the pool of orchestral players on which the concert life of London (and even the

---

1. The Indenture of Smart's apprenticeship is preserved in B.M., Add.Ms.41771, in which are other Indentures relating to boys apprenticed to Smart in 1799 (one being his brother, Thomas Robert) and 1830. Regarding his Freedom of the Grocers' Company, see Add.Ms.41772, f.8 v.

provinces) largely depended. He played either violin or viola and earned half a guinea a time. In the season 1794-5 he was engaged by J.P. Salomon for the orchestra which that impresario was to put at the disposal of Haydn, visiting England for the second time. On one never-to-be-forgotten day George Smart received instruction in the art of timpani playing from the master himself.

The regular timpanist having absented himself from rehearsal, Smart volunteered to take his place. Not being satisfied with his style of drumming Haydn left his place at the piano and came over to Smart to give practical demonstration of what he wanted. 'Oh, very well,' Smart said, 'we can do it like that in England if that's how you want it.'

At about this time Smart persuaded his father to publish

> *Divine Amusement; Being a Selection of the most admired Psalms, Hymns and Anthems used at St. James's Chapel for the Organ, Harpsichord and Piano Forte.... Composed and Compiled by George Thomas Smart, Organist of St James's Chapel And late one of the Children of His Majesty's Chapel Royal.*

A melody by Smart for Psalms XLVIII and CXXII (metrical) entitled 'Wiltshire' recalls family antecedents in that county. The melody 'Wheatfield' refers to Smart's visits to the Oxfordshire seat of Lord Charles Spencer and among the other composers admitted to the anthology is 'Hon. Mr Spencer' (see p.7), Smart's pupil. Smart did not reveal himself as a genius in composition, but his practical sense was well to the fore. Contrary to usual practice he tentatively completed the inner harmonies of his psalms and hymns, observing 'N.B. For the Accom[m]odation of those who do not understand through Bass it is Explained in Small Notes which may be Played, or Omitted at Pleasure.'

Smart also now began to take part in the Antient Concerts in a modest way. He sang among the basses and then in 1796 he was

> appointed to *turn over* for Joah Bates Esq., who was the *Conductor at the Organ*. I there took my 1st Lessons in conducting and ascertained the times in which Handel's music was performed, which probably Joah Bates might have heard in Handel's time...[2]

2. Add.Ms.41772, f.7. Joah Bates (1741-99) was the conductor of the Antient Concerts since their inception in 1776 and had directed the Handel Commemoration of 1784.

This apprenticeship to the Handelian tradition was to prove of considerable importance, for in due course Smart was to be considered as the authentic heir to the tradition.

By 1798 Smart was well established. On the musical side he had begun to build up a lucrative teaching practice which not only brought young ladies to his lodgings in large numbers but also took him into fashionable seminaries, as well as to 'preside at the harpsichord' both in the theatre and the concert-room. He was, in particular, engaged at Coleman's Theatre that year. In 'J. Denley's Concert' at which Thomas Greatorex – the leading conductor of the day – was 'at the Pianoforte' and in which Smart played the viola he appeared as a composer. Smart's glee *The Merry Gypsies*, first heard at Denley's Concert, was a popular item for some years to come.

Smart reckoned that his conducting career began in 1798 and that during the next 60 years he presided at some 1494 concerts. At the outset of his career, however, he maintained a strong interest in his other profession. His own master, Impey, had been druggist as well as grocer and Smart seems to have had a particular interest on this side. In 1802, in between conducting concerts at the Assembly Rooms in Edmonton, at Lady Dillon's, or Lady Buxton's,[3] and coping with an ever-growing list of fashionable pupils, he was 'taking lessons in Chemistry this year from Dr Gruber.' By now Smart owned a chaise, but he seemed accident-prone. In 1797 he had paid a surgeon at Islington 8/3, 'perhaps when my Horse fell into a drove of Pigs', and in 1802 he noted having been thrown out of his chaise. In that same year he went to France, together with his brother and his father.[4]

The times were out of joint. Even though it was possible to holiday in France the fact remained that England and France were on terms of mutual hostility. A patriot began to wonder in what way he could best serve his country and in 1803 Smart enlisted as a Lieutenant in the Royal Westminster Volunteers.[5] This commitment, however, did not interrupt the general flow of his activities. More and more the aristocracy

3. Lady Henrietta Dillon, wife of Viscount Dillon; Lady Buxton, wife of Sir Thomas Buxton Bt, of Runton, Norfolk.
4. Smart's account of this journey is contained in Add.Ms.41773.
5. Add.Ms.41771.

looked on him not only as a good music-master but also as an engaging dinner-guest. In 1805 he began a long, friendly, and profitable association with the Earl and Countess of Charleville, whose daughters he taught. On 25 February of that year Smart appeared at the New Musical Fund Concert solely as a composer, his 'new glee' – *Scenery by Moonlight* – sharing the novelty billing with a 'New Grand Symphony, never performed in England' by Beethoven. At the end of the year Smart, patriotic, composed the music for *An Acrostic Elegy on...Viscount Horatio Nelson*. Dining with Lady Hamilton, at Merton, two years later Smart made the acquaintance of the Second Earl Nelson, who was a frequent visitor at Merton. Soon after this Smart became acquainted with the Duke of Sussex (whose illegitimate daughter was his pupil), and acquaintance developed into firm friendship.

In the autumn of 1810 Smart was invited to the Charlevilles' Irish castle to give a concentrated course in music to the younger members of the family. He asked, and received, a fee of £100 9 0 to which, at the end of the course, the Earl and Countess made a 'present in addition' of ten guineas. His early education in commerce emboldened Smart – unlike most musicians – to ask a proper price for his services.

The idea that patronage of musicians by the nobility was reserved to the continent of Europe is one that does not quite stand up. The Irish peers, particularly, needed no instruction in the principles of feudalism, and occasionally one met with one who had the pretensions of an Esterházy. In 1807 the fourth Duke of Richmond and Lennox, after an adventurous career which included a duel with the Duke of York, was appointed Lord Lieutenant of Ireland. For six years the Richmonds lived in regal rather than vice-regal state. They have their place in one part of history on account of the ball given by them in Brussels on the eve of Waterloo. The Duke has a place in another because he conferred the honour of knighthood on George Smart.

As Lord Lieutenant, the Duke was empowered to dispose of certain honours – including that of knighthood – and he did so profitably. It took all that Smart earned from the Charlevilles to pay for the knighthood that the Duke mysteriously decided to confer on him. The details are in Smart's accounts:

| | |
|---|---|
| Aide de Camp (Capt. Shakespeare) | £10 10 0 |
| Ld. Lieut. Household | £51 10 8½ |
| King of Arms | £ 4 12 3½ |
| | 66 13 0 |

After that there was £52 to pay to the College of Heralds for a new coat of arms.[6] But it was worth it. To be Sir George by the age of 35 gave Smart a prestige enjoyed at that time of life by no other English musician either before or since.

Sir George spent more and more time in the best homes. In 1813 he began a long connection with the Hamiltons and the Argylls, and he was often a guest at Hamilton Palace and Inverary Castle. On 18 September, 1813, John Spencer wrote to Smart from Weymouth reporting a conversation with the Princess Charlotte – the daughter of the Prince of Wales.

SPENCER: I think your Royal Highness said you were acquainted with Sir George Smart
PRINCESS: Oh! Yes! I know him very well, and like him very much, he is such an excellent musician.[7]

In the same letter Spencer related how he had reminded the Princess how Sir George often 'plays and sings with the Duke of Sussex', and how he sometimes appeared at concerts at Carlton House.[8] The Princess, who fell out with her father over her refusal to marry the Prince of Orange, was one of the many members of the Hanoverian House to have found consolation in music. Smart arranged concerts for the Princess both before and after her marriage in 1816 to Leopold of Saxe-Coburg, and was greatly distressed at her tragic death in childbirth in 1817.[9]

Smart's friendship with the Duke of Sussex was similar to that, at a later point in history, between Sullivan and the Duke of Edinburgh.

6. Add.Ms.41772, f.26 v.
7. Add.Ms.41771.
8. See p. 10. Details relating to Smart's concerts at Carlton House, Kensington Palace, St James's Palace, etc., are contained in Add.Ms.41777.
9. Leigh Hunt commemorated the event in *His departed love to Prince Leopold*, which was set to music by Vincent Novello.

Smart was privileged not only to be the Prince's guest but also his host from time to time, and in 1811 he noted one day how his bill for giving dinner to the Prince amounted to £20 17 6 (including the wages of the cook). On 27 December 1818, Smart joined the Duke's household at Tunbridge Wells for a Christmas house-party. His expenses, he meticulously noted, were £2 18 6; but these were reduced by reason of his winning £1 4 0 from a Major Magrath at whist. It was through the Duke's recommendation – he being the Grand Master – that during that year Smart had succeeded Samuel Wesley as Grand Organist of the Grand Lodge of Freemasons. Smart had been a member of the Masonic Order since 18 June 1795.

In January 1822 Charles Knyvett, one of the organists of the Chapel Royal, died. Smart was appointed in his place. In March 1838 Thomas Attwood, Composer to the Chapel Royal, died. He was succeeded by Smart.

In 1793 a chaplain from the Electoral Court at Bonn had come to England as a refugee. Having arrived in Leicester he met William Gardiner, stocking manufacturer and amateur musician,[10] to whom he showed some chamber music by Ludwig van Beethoven that he had brought from Bonn. Thus it was that the E flat trio of 1792 had its first performance in England, in Leicester, in 1794. Five years later the first work by Beethoven to be published in England, *A Favourite Canzonetta, for the Piano Forte*, to words by William Wennington, was issued jointly by Broderip and Wilkinson and two other houses. It was, however, in 1813 that Beethoven's name first began really to appear prominent on the English musical scene. In that year the Philharmonic Society, of which Smart was a founder member, was instituted, and during the first season of its activities works by Beethoven were played at every concert.[11]

As in Handel's day there was at that time still held in London a Lenten season of oratorio. Its director from 1813 till 1825 was Smart (who also conducted the so-called 'City Concerts' in addition to many

10. See p. 46 n.8.
11. 8 and 15 March, and 21 June, symphonies; chamber music on 19 April, 3 and 17 May and 14 June, and the Finale of *The Men of Prometheus*. On 28 February 1814, the *Sinfonia Eroica* was performed for the first time at a Philharmonic Concert.

others). In his second season Smart introduced Beethoven's *The Mount of Olives* into the programme. This venture was very successful. The oratorio was performed ten times in London – at the Opera House in Drury Lane – and on 10 May 1814, also in Liverpool. An edition of the work, with a text modified to suit English theological prejudices and with the orchestral score reduced for use at the piano by Smart, was published by Chappell.

During the oratorio season of 1815 Smart performed the 'Battle Sinfonia' of Beethoven every night 'with the greatest applause' and for the Benefit of Widows of those soldiers who had fallen at Waterloo. On 6 April Smart conducted a New Musical Fund Concert for the first time and included the Battle Symphony. The programme thus enabled the audience to follow its course:

The Sinfonia commences with a March of the English Army to the Air of *Rule Britannia*; next follows a March of the French Army to the Air of *Marlbrook*: the Music then expresses the Battle between the two Armies, an Imitation of the Firing of Cannon and Musquetry, and the Retiring and Defeat of the French Army: a GRAND MARCH and INTRADA OF DRUMS and TRUMPETS announce the VICTORY: and concludes with 'GOD SAVE THE KING'; the Solos of which will be sung by the Principal Vocal Performers and Full Chorus.

*Two Military Bands will perform, and the Orchestra will be considerably augmented for this Piece.*[12]

At this time – through Charles Neate, the pianist, the Philharmonic Society was negotiating with Beethoven for three overtures to be written for the Society for a fee of 75 guineas. In response to this commission Beethoven sent the scores of *The Ruins of Athens*, *King Stephen*, and *Namensfeier* overtures. Of these only the last was a new work, and even that had already had its first performance.

In 1817 the overture to *Fidelio* was presented as a novelty at the first of the Season's Philharmonic Concerts on 24 February. For the seventh concert of this series parts of the Seventh Symphony were specially

12. Letters from J. Häring on behalf of Beethoven and from Beethoven himself to Smart are published in H. B. & C. E. E. Cox's *Leaves from the Journal of Sir George Smart*, London, 1907, pp. 49-54.

obtained from Germany. At this same concert – which began with a new symphony by Lord Burghersh[13] – Smart accompanied his pupil Miss Goodall, who also collaborated with him at the concerts he arranged for the Princess Charlotte, in a performance of *Adelaide*.

There was now further correspondence between the Philharmonic Society and Beethoven concerning an offer to him of a fee of 300 guineas to compose and direct the performance of two symphonies. Beethoven responded by proposing that the fee should be raised by 100 guineas, but in the end nothing happened in respect of this suggested commission.

Nevertheless the Philharmonic Society persisted and began a fresh bout of negotiation for a work to be composed expressly for the Society. It used as intermediary agents Cipriani Potter, who had met Beethoven in 1817, and Ferdinand Ries. Ries, a native of Bonn, had not only been Beethoven's pupil in Vienna, and remained his friend, but was the son of a celebrated Bonn musician who had been Beethoven's teacher and benefactor (see p. 54 n. 1). 'Young Ries,' married to an Englishwoman, a Director of the Philharmonic, and resident in London, was a close friend of Smart.

By now Smart,[14] also busy at every provincial centre, was the leading conductor in England. Gradually he began to be regarded as authoritative on Beethoven. On 24 April 1820 Smart conducted the *Eroica* (time taken in performance according to his own note, 41 minutes). On 26 February 1821 he conducted the Seventh; on 30 April the First, and on 28 May, the Sixth Symphonies (respectively taking 35 minutes, 25 minutes, and – with no cuts and no repeats – 37 minutes[15]). On 8 March 1824, Smart conducted a remarkable programme for the Philharmonic, which included Mozart's G minor Symphony (K.550), and Beethoven's *Egmont*, C minor Piano Concerto (Potter being the soloist), and Fourth Symphony. On 21 February 1825, he conducted the Fourth Symphony (31 minutes) and on 21 March in the same year directed the first English performance of the Ninth Symphony, in the Argyll Rooms. The

13. John Fane (1784-1859) who prior to succeeding to the Earldom of Westmorland was known as Baron Burghersh. See p. 24.
14. Smart conducted a Philharmonic Concert for the first time on 27 May 1816. He was conductor also on 19 June 1820, when Spohr was the 'Leader'.
15. Cf. performance of 5 May 1823: no repeats, 32 minutes.

soloists were Caradori, Goodall, Vaughan, and Phillips. The instrumental recitatives in the last movement were played as solos by Dragonetti, the most famous double-bass player of the age (see p. 27). This was the way in London until Dragonetti's death in 1846. This should have been the first performance of the work – 'geschrieben für die Philharmonische Gesellschaft in London'[16] – but it was not, an earlier performance having taken place in Vienna on 7 May 1824. Smart, understandably, was by no means satisfied with his reading of the work and decided to consult Beethoven in person.[17] As it happened he had already engaged to go to the continent with Charles Kemble – manager of Covent Garden, where Smart was music director – in order to discuss with Weber his commission to write a work – *Oberon* – for Covent Garden.

Sir George arranged to combine pleasure with business and to take three months off from his English affairs. By 7 August 1825, he and Kemble were in Cologne, staying at the Hotel de Mayence (see p. 30). Smart heard High Mass in the Cathedral, which he noted[18] 'is in a very unfinish'd state, [but] *if ever finish'd* it will be superior to every other...' He went on immediately to Bonn to enquire from Simrock, the music publisher, the whereabouts of Ferdinand Ries's father. He was directed to Godesberg, and having found the elder Ries was delightfully entertained by him. First there was an excursion to Rolandsworth. Then Smart partnered Ries in some of the latter's duets. After that the two of them 'jollified till 2 in the Morning'.

Smart journeyed comfortably up the Rhine, having had a preliminary meeting with Weber near Coblenz, and finally reached Vienna on 4 September. He stayed there until 20 September. At first he was shown round the city by 'young Ries', and introduced to Schuppanzigh, Mayseder, Czerny, and other musicians, as well as to Sir Henry Wellesley, the British Ambassador.[19]

16. Beethoven's autograph notes on the copy of the score of the Ninth Symphony in the possession of the Royal Philharmonic Society (B.M., R.P.S. 21).
17. '...a characteristic trait of zeal and energy', G. Hogarth, *The Philharmonic Society of London*, 1862, pp. 35-6.
18. The account of this three month excursion is contained in Add.Ms.41774.
19. Henry Wellesley (1773–1847) was the youngest son of the first Earl of Mornington (Garrett Colley Wellesley, 1735–81; see p. 37), and brother to the Duke of Wellington.

On Friday, 9 September, Holz[20] reported Beethoven's return from Baden and said he would be with his nephew at No. 72 Alleegasse. Smart then took prompt action

> ...at 12 took Ries to the Hotel Wilden Mann, Mr Schlesinger's (Music Seller at Paris) Lodgings, as I understood Mr Holtz Beethoven would be there and there I found him. He received me in the most pleasing manner – a numerous assembly of Professors to hear Beethoven's 2nd new M.S.Quartette bought by Mr Schlesinger [Op.132]. This Quartette is 3/4 of an hour in length – they played it twice. The 4 Performers were Schuppanzigh, Holtz, Weitz [added in pencil and should read Weiss], & Linke.
> *Most chromatic,* a slow movement subtitled – *praise for the recovery of an invalid* – Beethoven intended to allude to himself I suppose – he presided, took off his coat, and to express the staccato passages, took Mr Holtz's Violin and played this passage un peu hors de tone. I looked over the Score during the Performance – all paid him the greatest attention. About 14 were present...

Among those present were Beethoven's nephew, as well as Czerny, Bohm the violinist, and Marx, the cellist.

> I fix'd to go to Beethoven at Baden on Sunday – at 25m past 2, I left. had my hair cut – bought a hat...

On Sunday, 11 September, Smart went to Schlesinger's lodgings, where the old Abbé Stadler and Mlle Eskeles, a pupil of Moscheles, were among the company. Czerny, Schuppanzigh, and Linke, had just begun to play one of the Op.70 trios, the other coming after a repetition of the Op.132 Quartet. Schlesinger invited Smart to stay to dinner. Schuppanzigh – to whom Beethoven used playfully to refer as 'Sir John Falstaff' – sat at the head of the table.

> B. delightfully gay – but hurt that in the letter M[oscheles] gave me that his name should have been mixed with the other professors – however he soon got over it – he believes *I* do not [*lacuna*] that the high notes Handel wrote for Trumpets were played formerly perhaps so by one particular man – I gave him the oratorio Book & Bill – he

20. For Carl Holz see p.64 n.2.

invited me by his Nephew to Baden next Friday after Dinner he was coax'd to play extempore observing in French to me – 'What shall I play?' at the same time touching these notes

on which Theme he play'd for about 20 M. in a most extraordinary manner – appear'd much agitated when he rose, no one could be more agreeable than he was – plenty of jokes we all wrote to him by turns – but he can hear a little if you hollow [sic] quite close in his *left* Ear – a most delightful day...

On Friday Smart and Ries took a carriage – which cost them '5 F. in paper' – to Baden, and there they walked around a while until

we went to Beethoven's lodgings – curiously situated [in the Schloss Guttenbrunn] – a wooden Circus for Horsemanship created in a large court before his house – he has 4 large sized Rooms opening into each other, furnish'd a la genious [sic]. In one is the P.F. given him by Broadwood on which is written – besides the Latin line the Names of J. Cramer, Ferrari and C. Knyvett – Beethoven fully explain'd the times of his last Coral [sic] Sinfonia. Of the party present viz: Holtz, the Amateur Violin, C. Beethoven the Nephew (besides young Ries) agreed that the performance in Vienna only took 3/4 of an hour. B—n said not quite so much which I deemed to be totally impossible. It seems at Vienna the Recit was play'd only with 4 Celli and 2 Basses which certainly is better than having the tutti Bassi – We deservedly abused Reicha's specimen (Printed) of Fuging [sic][21] – he told me of a

21. Anton Reicha (1770-1836) was nephew of Joseph Reicha (1746-95), director of music in Bonn. An early friend of Beethoven he became an important theorist. He succeeded Méhul as director of the Paris Conservatoire. Smart referred, perhaps, to *Douze Fugues pour le Piano...dédiées aux Citoyens Méhul, Cherubini, le Sueur et Martini.*

Mass not yet printed he had composed – long conversation (in writing on my part) on musical subjects – very desirous to come to England.

Beethoven ordered dinner from his 'curious, old cook' and told his nephew Carl to see to the wine. Then

we all 5 took a walk – B. generally in advance humming some passage – he generally sketches his Subjects in the open Air. It was on one of these occasions Schuppanzigh told me he caught his deafness. He was writing in a garden and so absorb'd that he was not sensible of a pouring rain till his Music Paper was so wet that he could no longer write. From that day his deafness commenced which neither Art or time has cur'd. The waters at Baden whither he goes every summer has been of service to his Chest & Gout and his health is better than formerly – he would shew me Prince Charles beautiful Chateau in the Mountains [Weilburg des Erzherzogs Karl bei Baden] – also some Baths. On our return to Dinner at 2 – which was a most curious one and so plentiful that Dishes came in and we came out – for unfortunately we were in a hurry to get to the Stage by 4 – I gave him my Diamond Pin and he wrote me a droll Canon[22] – Unfortunately he had but 4 minutes to write it – we drank plenty of wine and he was very gay – I need not write down for Memory ever retains the events of this pleasurable day with Beethoven. His nephew regretted that they had no one to explain the profitable engagement offered to him by the Phil. last year.

We got back to Vienna about 7 in the Evening: I immediately went to bed exhausted with pleasure.

According to A. Thayer Beethoven had presented Hummel with the same canon some ten years earlier. Hence 4 minutes was ample time for Beethoven to write Smart's copy!

On the way to Dresden, Smart heard that Weber had died. Happily this was only rumour and Smart was able to enjoy a splendidly interesting week in the Saxon capital from 27 September. He saw *Der Freischütz* and *Euryanthe* and discussed Weber's forthcoming visit to London. From Dresden he travelled to Leipzig where Carl Friedrich Peters, the

22. Reproduced facsimile in Cox, *op. cit.*, between pp. 124 and 125.

publisher, told him some 'curious anecdotes' about Beethoven. He found Gottfried Christoph Härtel 'a very pleasant man [who] speaks English pretty well – has a list of London M. Sellers would do business with any of them. I took his Catalogues – he has many unpublish'd M.S. of S. Bach (some I saw) who resided in this town, of Haydn and Mozart – he supposes the best Sinfonia he ever wrote is lost – it was performed in the Town for a Benefit of Mozart'.

By the second week in October Smart had reached Berlin. Here he 'called on Mr Zelter...[who] shew'd me a M.S. Oratorio of Handel composed before he went to England – he has some studies of composition written by Handel'.[23] Zelter he described as a very unassuming man, who was proud of his plebeian origins and his early experiences as a worker on a building site. But the most memorable experience in Berlin was meeting the Mendelssohns. On 13 October 'young Mendelssohn play'd a clever Fugue and Pastorelle and Fantasia of S. Bach's all for the organ – with a part very difficult for the Pedals which his Sister play'd on the P.F.' Felix Mendelssohn also played a Kyrie and an overture of his own on his Broadwood piano. Years later Smart remembered how he became very intimate with Mendelssohn 'having made his acquaintance in Berlin in 1825. I then persuaded him to come to London. He gave me his M.S. Score of the Overture to "The Midsummer Night's Dream", which I had performed in London. It was an important Prelude to his arrival'.[24]

The two years that followed Smart's German tour were, in respect of the two musicians he had principally gone to meet, both mournful and memorable.

So far as Weber was concerned, despite the state of his health he looked forward greatly to visiting England and in anticipation took lessons in the English language. In this he made rapid progress.[25] On 5 March he arrived in London, where he was the guest of Smart at 91 Great Portland Street. For three months Weber enjoyed the plaudits of a generous public, and *Oberon* was played 28 times. The extant docu-

23. The reference may be to Handel's setting of B. H. Brockes's *Passion* composed in England in 1716, but fairly regularly performed in Hamburg for the next few years.
24. Letter to H. Lunn, 3 February 1864 (Add.Ms.40856, f. 123).
25. e.g. in two letters to Smart from Dresden, 4 January 1826 (Add.Ms.41771, f. 51).

ments show to what extent Smart dedicated himself to the task of making Weber's visit both a social and a financial success.

Before Weber left Dresden it was known that his tenure of life was to be short. The exertions and excitements of London were too much for a body racked with tuberculosis. Weber died at Smart's house during the night of 4-5 June. On 12 June Smart conducted the last Philharmonic Concert of the season. It began with 'Handel's Dead March in Saul, as a tribute to Departed Genius.' Nine days later all the leading musicians of London joined together to pay tribute to Weber at the funeral service at the Moorfields Roman Catholic Chapel. Smart was the chief mourner. Mozart's Requiem was performed by the most distinguished artists, with Thomas Attwood – once a pupil of Mozart – at the organ. The funeral expenses amounted to £188 and were entirely borne by the professional musical fraternity of London.

On 12 February, 1827, Beethoven was in deep distress. He had quarrelled violently with his nephew. He had survived an attack of pneumonia, but was being inexorably and painfully propelled towards death by cirrhosis of the liver. He was in the grip of poverty, but also of inspiration. He thought on the Tenth Symphony that was never to be accomplished. He hoped, perhaps, that the English might help him, and so he wrote to Moscheles enclosing a letter to Smart. 'I remember,' he wrote to the latter,

that some years ago the Philharmonic Society proposed to give a concert for my benefit. This prompts me to request you, dear Sir, to say to the Philharmonic Society that if they be now disposed to renew their offer it would be most welcome to me. Unhappily since the beginning of December I have been confined to bed with dropsy – a most wearing malady the result of which cannot yet be ascertained. As you are already well aware, I live entirely by the produce of my brains, and for a long time to come all idea of writing is out of the question. My salary is in itself so small, that I can scarcely contrive to defray my half-year's rent out of it. I therefore entreat you kindly to use all your influence for the furtherance of this project; your generous sentiments towards me convincing me that you will not be offended by my application. I intend also to write to Herr Moscheles on this subject, being persuaded that he will gladly unite with you in promoting my object. I am so weak I can no longer write so I only dictate this. I hope, dear Sir, that you will soon cheer me by an answer, to say whether I may look forward to the fulfilment of my request.

In the meantime, pray receive the assurance of the high esteem with which always remain, etc. etc....

Not having had any reply Beethoven wrote again to Moscheles on 14 March, but four days later he was overjoyed to receive a gift of £100 from the Philharmonic Society, which had acted with great expedition. On 19 March Smart conducted the Fifth Symphony at a Philharmonic Concert.[26] A week later Beethoven was dead.

On 17 April Smart had a letter from Anton Schindler, written on 2 April:

...He requested me, when he should be no more, to offer his warmest & most grateful thanks to you & Mr Stumpff,[27] and thro' your medium to the Philharmonic Society & the whole English Nation for the attentions & friendships shown him during his life, & more especially towards the close – I hasten to acquit myself of this last & earnest desire of my deceased friend, & by you Sir George to make known in London there, the sentiments of our immortal Beethoven....His place of interment is at Währing, a village situated near Vienna, where his remains repose near those of the lamented Lord Ingestre...[28]

The reputation of Beethoven having been firmly established in England, Sir George pursued his general activities with undiminished zeal. He

26. Smart noted '31 minutes'. In March 1830, however, he got through the work in 26 minutes. He was precise in indicating the overall time of performance of works, but he almost always omitted to refer to repeats or cuts (the only exceptions being those shown on p. 10).

27. Johann Andreas Stumpff (1769-1846), a native of Ruhla in Thuringia, was a musician and a harp manufacturer. He settled in London where he lived for forty years or so and made a considerable fortune. Stumpff was a friend of Goethe and in 1824 he travelled to Vienna in order to make the acquaintance of Beethoven. Beethoven, who called Stumpff '...mein guter deutscher Engländer', hoped that his nephew Carl might go to England, where Stumpff would look after him, in order to learn English. Nothing, however, came of this. In 1826 Stumpff presented Beethoven with the volumes of Arnold's edition of the works of Handel. (See Frimmel, II, pp. 271-80).

28. Add.Ms.41771, f. 81. Charles Thomas Talbot, Viscount Ingestre (1802-26), was the eldest son and heir of Earl Talbot of Hensol (Lord Lieutenant of Ireland, 1817-21). Educated at Eton and Christ Church, Oxford, he died in Vienna.

had a great faith in the future as well as respect for the past and addressed himself to both in a truly English pragmatic manner. The undisputed festival director of the age, Smart covered the length and breadth of Britain in furtherance of the cause of the propagation of musical truth. He took over the choral tradition – the 'Handelian' tradition – from Bates and Greatorex and released it from its middle-class moorings. Especially in the north of England he strengthened claims to choral excellence by drawing on the reserves of energy and imagination of the working class. The list of festivals conducted by Smart[29] reads as a gazetteer of the British Isles. Some places were more important than others, but wherever he went Smart was gratefully received. In Dublin they made him a Freeman of the City. The same honour was accorded to him in Norwich – where he instituted the Norwich and Norfolk Festival – and he was also given the honour of Life Governorship of the General Hospital.

In London Smart controlled the music for royal occasions, including that for the funerals of George IV and William IV and for the Coronations of William IV and Victoria. He directed the programmes for the Public Anniversary Dinners of the Covent Garden Theatrical Fund,[30] and occasionally introduced into them music of an older dispensation – such as Bennet's *All creatures now are merry-minded*. He was in charge of the musical entertainments given in the City on Lord Mayor's Day, and of the annual Festival of the Sons of the Clergy. In 1834 the last of the great Handel celebrations held in Westminster Abbey took place. Smart was the conductor. He was also a professor at the Royal Academy of Music which had been founded – largely through the insistence of Lord Burghersh – in 1822.

Whenever he could be of service to the young Smart exerted himself. In 1824 he conducted a performance of a Hummel concerto at Drury Lane in which the soloist was the thirteen-year-old Liszt. In 1829 he greeted Mendelssohn on his arrival in London and treated him with charming consideration. At a party at which Mendelssohn and Smart were both present their hostess asked Sir George if he would play the piano. 'No, no,' he said, 'don't call upon the old post-horse when you

29. Contained in Add.Ms.34278.
30. Founded in 1765.

18

have a high-mettled young racer at hand.'[31] The 'high-mettled young racer' became the darling of the concert-going public and the hostesses of Kensington. The *Midsummer Night's Dream* overture which Sir George had heard with such interest in Berlin was performed at a morning concert in July in aid of the victims of the recent floods in Silesia. The Philharmonic Society included it in the programme of the first concert of the next season. Smart continued to watch over the fortunes of Mendelssohn and on 7 October, 1836, gave the first English performance of *St. Paul* at St Peter's Church, Liverpool, during the Liverpool Musical Festival.

The most important Festival that Smart directed so far as his private life was concerned was that at Derby in 1831. Smart had long since known that at a provincial Festival it was advisable to be on the best of terms with the influential people of the neighbourhood. It most towns the Mayor and the Vicar were dignitaries whose good will was invaluable. In Derby in 1831 both offices were held by the same individual.

The Rev. Charles Stead Hope (1762–1841), the son of the Vicar of All Saints', having been educated at Derby and Harrow Schools and St John's College, Cambridge, assumed a curacy at St Werburgh's Church, Derby, in 1785. Twelve years later he was appointed Vicar of All Saints, which position he held for 44 years. He held other cures simultaneously and also found time to devote to local secular affairs, and was five times Mayor of Derby. Hope's daughter, Frances Margaret, 29 in 1831, was unmarried and living at home.

Armed with letters of introduction from Charles Knyvett and others, Smart reached Derby at the end of September and immediately presented himself to the Vicar-Mayor (the nearest English equivalent to an Archbishop-Elector). It so happened that Smart was concerned about his servant – a man named W.Hall – who had hurt his shoulder. Accustomed to proffer her services whenever acts of mercy were called for, the Vicar's daughter, Margaret, took control of the situation and superintended Hall's recovery. Accustomed to the energy and efficiency of her father she noted with approval that Sir George was a man of the same type.

It was a big, ambitious, music meeting after the pattern of a Three

31. *The Mendelssohn Family*, ed. S. Hensel, London 1881. 2 vol., I, p.229.

Choirs Festival, with the bulk of the performances taking place in All Saints' Church. The principal patron was the Duke of Devonshire, who, true to type, brought his party into the hall at the Second Concert after the 'Jupiter' Symphony had started. The sermon at the Morning Service on 27 September was preached by a member of the ducal family, the Hon. and Rev. Augustus Cavendish, and, Smart noted, it lasted for 40 minutes. At the Third Concert Smart, who still 'presided at the Piano-Forte', directed Beethoven's First Symphony. But the main interest centred on the fashionable 'Chevalier' Neukomm, one of the most prolific oratorio-purveyors of the age. On 28 September Neukomm conducted the first performance of *The Mount Sinai*, during which Smart sat with the Mayor in his pew. This oratorio was followed by copious excerpts from Handel, the whole session lasting from 11am until 3.14pm.

Although much occupied in the details of the Festival Smart made good use of his free time. So on 28 February 1832 he married Margaret Hope at Richmond, the wedding being conducted by the Sub-dean of the Chapel Royal. The marriage was a singularly happy one and, as Fanny and Sophy Horsley, and Arthur Sullivan testified, Lady Smart was a woman of charm, intelligence, and great kindness. In later years the Smarts enjoyed visiting Derbyshire,[32] where Lady Smart had numerous relatives and was well known. In July 1844 while guests of the Rev. R. M. Hope, they made an excursion to Ashbourne 'to look at Handel's works, belonging to the Rev. Court Granville, Calwich Hall.'[33]

That was the year in which Smart made his last public appearance at a Philharmonic Concert. The concert which took place on 25 March showed signs of changing values, since the Court pianist from Saxe-Coburg-Gotha who was the guest artist played 'part' of Chopin's First Piano Concerto. The programme otherwise contained Spohr's E flat Symphony, Weber's *Ruler of Spirits* and Cherubini's *Médée* overtures, and Beethoven's Eighth Symphony.

By this time the Beethoven cult in England had been strengthened at

32. See reference to the Matlock countryside on p. 40.
33. Handel's friend Bernard Granville inherited the family estate at Calwich, Staffs. The manuscript copies of works by Handel which were given to Granville remained in the family until 1915 when they were acquired for the British Museum.

every point. The Philharmonic Society had done its work well. Sir George, active in so many concert-giving organisations in London, had made a great contribution both in the capital and in the provinces. Where people outside of London knew the orchestral works of Beethoven they did so because of Smart's initiative.

It had not always been easy. Then as now the outside edges of modernity in music were approached by the controlling authorities with some caution. Smart had wanted to conduct a trial performance of the Choral Symphony for the Philharmonic in 1828, in which he could demonstrate what he had learned concerning its interpretation from Beethoven. The idea of such a performance was dropped on account of cost. Smart conducted the symphony, however, at a Benefit for Neate in 1830 – after which Moscheles became its chief exponent, giving a notable performance in 1838.

The Violin Concerto was played at a Philharmonic Concert in 1832 but did not arouse much interest until given by Joachim at a Philharmonic Concert conducted by Mendelssohn in 1844. The first complete performance of *Fidelio* in London took place at the King's Theatre in 1832. It was in that year that Thomas Alsager, a proprietor of *The Times* and an ardent music-lover, promoted a private performance of the *Missa solemnis*, which Moscheles was engaged to conduct. This performance was otherwise noteworthy on account of Clara Novello, then only fourteen years old, taking part.[34]

As the publicity for a Beethoven memorial was warmed up so did interest in London increase. On 9 March 1845 Moscheles played a strenuous programme of piano sonatas for an 'Offering to Beethoven'. Later that month 'Beethoven Illustrative Parties' were promoted by the Queen Square Select Society – a brain-child of Alsager, who in 1845 also founded a Beethoven Quartet Society.

The desire to raise a permanent memorial to Beethoven in his native city – the development of which is discussed in the following chapter – led to a sequence of ideas and events that before long worked itself into the pattern of English musical affairs.

34. In his list of pupils for 1830-1 Smart included 'Miss Novello, *gratis* – V. Novello's daughter.'

# CHAPTER 2

# The determination of Dr Breidenstein

In his famous Bach biography J.Nikolaus Forkel made it clear to German musical scholars how they could effectively serve the father-land. In the half-century that followed Forkel's death in 1818 there were many opportunities for such scholars so to justify themselves. During the years that lay between the War of Liberation of 1813 and the Franco–Prussian War of 1870 the inculcation of a due reverence for national heroes was a matter not only of pedagogic but also of political concern. Among those who qualified as national heroes the most eminent musicians of the German tradition won the highest regard. More, perhaps, than others of the illustrious dead they symbolised the ideal of national unity, for music was considered as the national art.

In 1820 the body of Josef Haydn was taken with due ceremonial from Vienna to Eisenstadt where the Bergkirche became virtually a Haydn monument, while the town itself became a place of pilgrimage for Haydn lovers. In the autumn of 1842 a campaign which had gone on for some years reached its successful conclusion when the Mozart monument in the Mozartplatz in Salzburg was unveiled during the first Mozart Festival. In the following year, largely through Mendelssohn's persistence, the Bach monument outside the Thomaskirche in Leipzig also was unveiled in the course of an impressive ceremony. In 1844, thanks to Richard Wagner, Weber's remains were returned to Dresden from London and a year later the movement for a suitable memorial began to gather impetus (see p. 113). Fourteen years passed, and then, during a festival of his music, the statue of Handel in the Market Place in Halle was handed over to the city. To all of these operations, except the first, British musicians and well-wishers lent their aid.

Heinrich Carl Breidenstein (1796-1876) belonged to the first generation of musical scholars after Forkel, and was one of the founders of the profession of musicology. A native of Steinau in Hesse he studied law and philology in Berlin and Heidelberg, after which he was a pupil of Hegel and Schleiermacher in philosophy. His music tutors were Anton Thibaut and J.C.H.Rinck, the Court organist in Darmstadt. In 1822 Breidenstein was appointed Music Director in the University of Bonn, which had been established four years earlier and was accommodated in the former Electoral palace. His inaugural lecture was on the theme, 'The present condition of musicology'. After a year he became a *Privatdozent* and in 1826 was raised to the rank of Professor. Nothing if not conscientious Breidenstein immediately took a sabbatical year and pursued a further course of study in Berlin, where he became acquainted with the Mendelssohns. Breidenstein gained a reputation as a good teacher – his pupils at one time or another included Albert, to be Prince Consort of England, and Max Bruch – and he founded an orchestral society in Bonn in 1843.

It was, however, the death of Beethoven that fired Breidenstein with his main ambition – to see to it that in the city of his birth there was a fitting monument to Bonn's most famous son. Already in 1828 he had raised the matter with various persons of influence, but immediate action was prevented by a serious outbreak of cholera.

In the course of the next few years, however, a committee was assembled with A.W.Schlegel, Professor of Literature and one of the most distinguished of Shakespeare scholars, as Secretary. The committee included J.J.Noeggerath, a mineralogist, P.F.von Walther, a physician, Count Carl Egon von Fürstenberg, a member of the Prussian Royal Household, as well as other academics and local worthies. The only musician who was a member was Breidenstein.

On 17 December 1835, a general Appeal for funds to make possible the erection of a Beethoven monument was issued by the Bonn Committee. The Crown Prince of Prussia (who succeeded to the throne as Friedrich Wilhelm IV in 1840) signalled his good wishes, while from Düsseldorf Prince Friedrich sent a contribution. The King of Bavaria,

Ludwig I, also supported the proposal to honour Beethoven's memory and having attended a concert organised to raise funds expressed himself as especially delighted with a performance of the *Fidelio* overture on four pianos.

In England, the cause of a foreign musician always being dear to native hearts, the Appeal was scrutinised with friendly concern. It had powerful advocates. Leading them was Lord Burghersh. Burghersh, who had studied music at Cambridge but who was by profession a high-ranking diplomat, had been largely responsible for the foundation of the Royal Academy of Music. Acquainted with musicians all over Europe – he had been a pupil of Mayseder in Vienna – Burghersh was an indispensable ally in any musical undertaking. In 1841, in which year he became British Ambassador to Berlin, he succeeded to the title of Earl of Westmorland. Supporting Burghersh was Ignaz Moscheles, who had known Beethoven in the early part of the century and had arranged the piano score of *Fidelio* at his request. Moscheles, who made his home in London in 1826, became a Director of the Philharmonic Society in 1832.

In March 1837 the *Morning Post* (quoted by the *Musical World*) stated 'There are two compositions for which every person is asking; – we mean Spohr's Sinfonia "The Power of Sound" and Beethoven's Sinfonie Characteristique "The Passion of Joy". We take it for granted, they both will be done during the present season.' The writer complained that the Directors of the Philharmonic had been dragging their feet, scared from performing the Ninth Symphony on account of its length and the costs incurred. Nevertheless it was duly performed, conducted by Moscheles, on 17 April. Then came a letter from Schlegel, from Bonn, soliciting contributions for his fund. Moscheles, William Knyvett, Smart, and Burghersh decided that a 'grand concert' should be organised to raise money for the appeal. The artists taking part, of couse, would give their services.

*The Musical World* approved a note in *The Times* which it reprinted:

England…where so great an impulse has recently been given to musical studies of the most refined and perfect description, ought not to remain content into following in the wake of a German town, whatever glory it may have acquired by having been the birthplace of Beethoven, in a tribute of this sort to talent which is no where better understood or more justly appreciated. But it is not too late; the hint thus seasonably given, and promptly acted upon, England may also contain a 'monument to Beethoven'.[1]

As it happened the time was not quite propitious for a concert, for King William IV had died in June, and this had thrown the town into disarray. Apart from this, however, the date decided on, 19 July, was too late in the season, so that while 'the members of the Ancient Concert orchestra came forward to a man...the Lord and Lady subscribers turned their backs on the affair'. Those who had recently flocked to hear 'an unknown oratorio by a nearly unknown composer' (St. Paul, by Mendelssohn) quite neglected Beethoven.

It was, nonetheless, a splendid occasion so far as the music was concerned. The 'Ancient Music', the Philharmonic, the managements of the Operas at Covent Garden and Drury Lane, pooled their resources. Schroeder-Devrient joined a fine list of English vocalists, and the conducting was shared by Smart, Moscheles, and Knyvett. The first part of the programme consisted of *The Mount of Olives*; the second, of the Choral Symphony, which Moscheles conducted; the third, of *Egmont*, the 'Emperor' (with Moscheles as soloist), and excerpts from *Fidelio*.

Despite all the difficulties that had been encountered the concert raised a little more than £50, which was duly forwarded to Bonn. (On 24 July Smart noted that he had sent an independent contribution of two guineas to the fund through Greatorex.) The event brought a cautionary footnote and a sideways glance at the English manner of commemorating another great master.

...The greatest monument Beethoven can have is the proper performance of his works: the annual repetition of the choral symphony by 1000 or 1500 persons - the grand masonic hymn of Europe upborne by 1000 voices, and supported by an orchestra of 500 instrumentalists, would be the apotheosis which even the composer would have desired for an extension of his thread of life to have witnessed.[2]

1. *The Musical World*, VI, no. LXX, July 14 1837, p. 79.
2. *The Musical World*, ibid. pp. 91–2.

While the English, even though their financial contribution as yet was modest, showed a commendable enthusiasm for the memorial project, the French, for reasons which were understandable and were to obtrude themselves later (see p. 82), were less than luke-warm. Cherubini was keen but a whip-round among the Beethoven lovers of Paris produced only £17. Concluding that an act of faith would prove a valuable stimulus at this point, the German committee firmly gave it out on 20 April 1839, that the Beethoven monument was definitely to be erected in the Münsterplatz in Bonn. At this juncture Liszt was brought onto the committee and one of his first contributions to its deliberations was a proposal that the monument should be sculpted in marble by his friend Lorenzo Bartolini. He wrote to Bartolini and reported in November that a statue could be finished within two years at a cost of between 50,000 and 60,000 francs. He wrote to his mistress the Comtesse d'Agoult, on 17 December, observing that since the committee already had 40,000 francs in the bank raising the rest of the money required would be easy.[3]

The Bonn members of the committees, however, were not enthusiastic about Liszt's proposal. They wrote to him drawing attention to the magnificent bronze statues with which Thorwaldsen had enriched Germany, citing particularly that of Gutenberg in Mainz, and of which in any case the costs compared more than favourably with Bartolini's estimate. Having turned down Liszt's proposal – which was the first of many disagreements between him and his fellow organisers – the committee set up a small consultative body of experts: von Schadow, Director of the Düsseldorf Art Gallery, with two Düsseldorf colleagues; Welke, Professor of Archaeology at Bonn; de Lassaulx, Building Inspector in Coblenz; and de Noël, a Bonn gentleman of independent means.

On 10 February 1842, E. J. Hähnel of Dresden was chosen to design the statue of Beethoven and asked to agree to a contract requiring completion of the work by 6 August 1843. That was to be a special date in

3. The money in hand had been largely raised by special concerts in Aachen, Augsburg, Berlin (Singakademie), Breslau, Cassel, Coblenz, Cöthen, Cologne, Danzig, Darmstadt, Dessau, Dresden, Erfurt, Mainz, Merseburg, München, Prague, Stettin, and other smaller towns. In Cassel, Ludwig Spohr was responsible for the 'Beethoven Monument' concerts.

the history of Germany, for on it was to be celebrated the 'Thousand Year *Reich*'.[4] Hähnel, however, required more time for his commission, and asked for another two years.

In the event the summer of 1845 was the more suitable from many points of view, not least because then there would be no other similar and conflicting events. When 1845 arrived, Breidenstein began to collect his forces for the occasion, singers being invited from the societies that normally supported the choirs of the Lower Rhine Festival, and orchestral players from a much wider area. The orchestra eventually contained expatriate Germans from France, Belgium, and Holland. Heading the double basses was the great Dragonetti, now 82 years old, from London, who had been friendly with Haydn, and also with Beethoven. The choir for the Festival numbered 343 singers and Franz Weber, from Cologne, was appointed chorus-master, while the orchestra comprised 162 players. Liszt was invited to write one work in honour of the occasion, while Breidenstein considered that he too should make an original contribution.

It was hoped that Ludwig Spohr, one of the greatest conductors of that era, would be able to conduct some part of the Festival. In view of what had happened in 1842, however, there was no certainty that Spohr would be able to accept the invitation. In 1842 the Co-Elector of Hesse-Darmstadt, Spohr's employer, had refused him permission to conduct a work of his own at the Norwich Festival in spite of one request having been made on behalf of the Festival by the British Foreign Office and another, and more personal one, by the Duke of Cambridge.

On 26 July 1845, Spohr went to Berlin for the first performance of his last opera, *Die Kreuzfahrer*, after which he received through Alexander von Humboldt an invitation to dine with the King (Friedrich Wilhelm IV) and Queen. After dinner Spohr was fêted by the court orchestra and presented with a laurel wreath in gold. Such was the esteem in which he was held outside of his own principality. But whether he would be able to go to Bonn was for some time in doubt:

Scarcely had *Spohr* returned to Cassel than he was again upon the move, and

---

4. The division of the Carolingian Empire at Verdun in 843 left most of the German territories east of the Rhine as a single entity under the rule of 'Ludwig the German'.

this time to Bonn, where on the 11th of August the inauguration of the monument to *Beethoven* was to be celebrated. To the invitation that had been sent to him many weeks before, to conduct a portion of the musical perform-ance upon the occasion, he had at first, it is true, replied declining it, as a special leave of absence would have been necessary for him to proceed thither, and after having already applied for one the year before to direct the Brunswick musical festival[5] he did not like to make a similar application so soon. It was however shortly announced to him in a second letter, that the committee of the festival having been informed that the Prince was then staying in Cologne for a few days, they had despatched a deputation thither to invite him and the Countess *Schaumburg* to the approaching ceremony in her native town of Bonn, and to solicit at the same time a leave of absence for *Spohr*, which had been graciously granted. As no further obstacle had intervened, *Spohr* lost no time in proceeding thither, to lend his personal assistance at the grand festival, which had drawn together from far and near the musical youth of Germany, to do honour to the great master whose memorial was to be inaugurated.[6]

Spohr arrived in Bonn on 6 August and went straight to the Goldener Stern (the favourite hotel of the British Royal Family) where a room had been reserved. Liszt had come to the Rhineland several weeks before, in order to attend the meetings of the Beethoven Committee, to rehearse his cantata and to deal with the detractors.[7] Since he stayed with friends in Cologne, however, he was not much seen in Bonn. He managed a weekly rehearsal of the Cantata, but was seldom to be seen at committee meetings.

Meanwhile, oblivious of the politics of German music, Sir George Smart had received and replied to his invitation to attend the Festival.

5. Spohr conducted a performance of the oratorio *Der Fall Babylons* at a festival held in his honour in Brunswick, in the vicinity of which city he had been born and where he was educated.

6. *Louis Spohr's Autobiography*, trans. from the German, London, 1865, p. 270.

7. On 28 April 1845, Liszt wrote of his cantata to the Abbé de Lamarnais, that 'the text, at any rate, is tolerably new; it is a sort of *Magnificat* of human genius conquered by God in the eternal revelation through time and space – a text which might apply equally well to Goethe or Raphael or Columbus, as to Beethoven . . .'

On 23 July he wrote to Gaetana Belloni how '. . . Bonn is in a flutter since I arrived, and I shall easily put an end to the paltry, underhand opposition which had been formed against me . . .'

London No 91 Gt Portland St
July 12th 1845

Sir,

I beg to acknowledge the receipt of a letter dated Bonn July 1st from the Committee for the Beethoven Monument; I consider myself much honored by their invitation which I accept with great pleasure, for it will afford me the high gratification of being present upon so interesting an occasion as the Inauguration of the Statue in honor of Beethoven on August the 11th next.

I hope to be allowed to pay my respects to you in person at Bonn about August the 7th.

I have the honor to be
Sir
Your most obedient Servt.
G.S.
Organist & Composer to Her Majesty's Chapels Royal.

To Dr Breidenstein, President
of the Committee of the Beethoven Monument.
on the Envelope

Sr Hochwohlgebon Dr Herrn Dr
Breidenstein etc etc etc Bonn

by favor of Mr Jos. Ries.[8]

Smart gave the letter to Joseph Ries, who was going to Bonn, to deliver to Breidenstein in person.

8. Copy of letter in Add. 41776 f. 74.

Pieter Joseph Ries (1791-1882) was younger brother to Ferdinand. He was an amateur musician and resident in London where he was foreign correspondent to Broadwoods. He had been previously employed by the East India Company and was a friend of Charles Lamb.

# CHAPTER 3

# Preparations for a journey

Sir George Smart had a reputation for thoroughness. From the notes which enclose his diary of his journey in 1845 it is clear that this reputation was well deserved and that it related not only to his musical activities. Thus we read from folio 84 of his manuscript, working backwards:

> Hotel l'Allemande-Ostende recommended by Lady Westmoreland
> Mr Jos. Ries recommends Hotel des Bains at Ostende.[1] Le Chev
> [alier] Hebeler [see p.31] recommends the Hotel Grand Monarque at
> *Aix la Chapelle.* Mr Jos Ries recommends Hotel de Trèves at Bonn[2]
> and he recommends at Cologne Hotel de Vienne (Glockengasse
> No 6 or 8

> When I was at Cologne in August 1825 we lodged at Hotel de
> Mayence – A good Hotel [see p.11].

> *Malines* – Hotel de la Grand Place
> Liege. Fagot-Ionniaux. Hotel de Hollande

1. In *Der Passagier im Königreich Belgien* (Berlin, 1845) the recommended hotels in Ostend were Hotel des Bains (rue du Quai), Hotel de Flandre (rue du Chat), and Hotel du Lion d'or (specially recommended to German guests).
2. 'Hotel de Treves, a clean and comfortable moderate house', *Bradshaw's Illustrated Hand-Book for Travellers in Belgium*, etc. (London, 1855); 'Hotel de Traves – J.L. Waldschmidt. Facing the Town-Hall, and characteristic Market Place. Table d'hôte at 1 p.m., first-rate French cookery. Good attendance and reasonable charges. English spoken. Advantageous arrangements for the winter', *A Practical Rhine Guide by An Englishman Abroad* (London, 1857).

Jean Marie Farina. Vis à vis la Place Juliens-*a Cologne* le plus ancien Distillateur de l'Eau de Cologne.

Smart was given the address of the Farinas by Joseph Ries, who acted as their agent in Britain.

f. 83v

    Chambre No. 16 Hotel de Treves – Bonn
            No. 14 Mr Robertson's[3]
    Jonas Cahn – Banker – BOURR
    Vigilant (Cab) Fare 1 Franc
    in Cologne – the Fare is 10 Grots. 1d English
    Mr le Conseilleur Wegeler – ⎫
    Beethoven's Friend[4]       ⎭
    Dr Breidenstein President of Committee
    No. 929 B – Belderberg
    Mr [Franz Anton] Ries – am Neugass Belderberg.
    Head Waiter – 'Ober Kellner' – 6 Groschen per day
    Mr Eisin – Fredrich Wilhelm Strasse 2, Cologne sells Panorama Views
    of Bonn & asks 3 Frans each.

Folio 83 remained blank, but good use was made of those following.

f. 82.

|  | £ s d |
|---|---|
| 1845 Previous Expences | 2 |
| July 15 – This Book at Kirton's | |
|    16 Passport at The Prussian Consul's | |
| Office Le Chev. Hebler [sic] No. 106 | |
| Fenchurch St.[5] | 7 |
|    18 Kirton for Tablet on Foreign | |
| Monies | 2 6 |
| Letter of Invitation for Dr Breidenstein | |
|                  Postage | 8 |

3. See p. 35.
4. Franz Gerhard Wegeler, a doctor in Bonn, was a lifelong friend of Beethoven and co-author with F. Ries of *Biographische Notizen über Ludwig van Beethoven* (Koblenz, 1838). Wegeler was married to Eleonore von Breuning.
5. Chevalier B. Hebeler was a principal in Messrs B. Hebeler & Co. of 106 Fenchurch Street.

26 Letter from Jos.Ries received at Hythe                                    1  4
27 Postage from Hythe to Mr Simrock at Bonn, to
acknowledge Mr Jos.Ries having secured the 2 Rooms            1  3
31 To *meet* Mr Jos.Ries *at Dover*. Omnibus 1 Horse
from Hythe to Folk-stone at 20 m to 10 morning & got
to Folk-stone Train to Dover 25 m to 11                              1  6
Train from Folk-stone to Dover got there at 11 *morning*.    1  6

f. 82v.

Recommended by Mr Robertson for Tooth Powder 'Camphorate
Myrrh' sold at Stringer's next to Northumberland House-Strand

For Rubbing
    Pair of Gloves & Belt – at Dinniford's – Chemist,
    Old Bond St. Cost about 15s

I like 'Geissenheimer' 20 Gros per 1 Bottle which we drank
at 'Hotel de Vienne' Cologne

'Pisporter' at 15 Gros. per Bottle is a good Wine which we
drank at Hotel de Treves, Bonn
July 31 continued)                              brought up         17  9
Dinner at Diver's Dover Castle Hotel in the Harbour          3  6
Jos.Ries landed from Ostend about 1/4 to 5, left
Ostend about 9 Morning – wind against them. He landed
in a Boat near the York Hotel.
Railway at ½ past 6 Evening from Dover to Folk-stone
got there at 1/4 to 7                                                          1  6

Several pages of Smart's notebook are occupied by details of money
exchange (see Appendix 1) after which preliminary information relating
to continental travel is noted:

f. 5v

August 1845 The Train *Stop*
(where Refreshments can be procured) at
Maline for ½ or 3/4 of an hour,
waiting for the Train from Bruxelles or
Antwerp – N.B. They change *Carriages*

at Maline likewise at Verviers,
therefore look after the *luggage*
The Trains also *stop* at *Verviers*
and at *Aix la Chapelle* for ½ or 3/4 of an hour
The Passport will be taken at Ostend ⎫
get it back *in time* to depart by the Train. ⎭
The Passport will be taken at *Verviers* or
*Herbesthal* – ask for it at
*Aix la Chapelle.*

f.6

The Government Packets leave Ostend every day
*except Saturdays* at 8 in the morning:— there is a train
every morning: leaves Ghent at ½ past 5 and arrives at
Ostende about ½ past 7 in time for the departure of the
Packet which waits for the Letters by this Train.

Regarding money for the expedition Smart recorded:

f.6v

| | |
|---|---|
| Took——— in Gold, Silver & Copper | £20 |
| In Paper Notes | £15 |
| | —— |
| | £35 |

10 £ Note
    HB No 61349, London, June 10, 1845
        N. Richton [?]
    on the back. Coutts & Co – July 16. 45

5 £ Note
    HC No. 42346 London May 13. 1845
        J. Nantin [?]
    On the back G. Strickland Esq.

Left at Hythe with Margaret August 4th 1845

| | | |
|---|---|---|
| 1 Note of | £5 | |
| Sovereigns | £9 | 10 |
| Silver | | 10 8 |
| | £15 | 8 |

Sir George and Lady Smart travelled to Hythe on 19 July. They had reserved rooms there for eight weeks (until 6 September) with a Mrs Love. Mrs Love's charges for the eight weeks amounted to sixteen guineas, to which were added further expenses of £28 3 0. While he was in Hythe Sir George called on the surgeon Fagg, son of the surgeon in Ashford who had befriended him as a boy.

While Sir George accomplished his grand tour, Margaret waited in Hythe, where a regular flow of letters kept her informed as to what was going on.

# CHAPTER 4

# With Sir George to Cologne

At Dover Smart picked up his travelling companion, Henry Robertson, the Treasurer of Covent Garden Theatre, who was going to Bonn for the Festival and then on to Italy with his nephew. Robertson was a friend of Vincent Novello and Leigh Hunt, and a keen musical amateur. He was immortalised by Leigh Hunt in his sonnet, *To Henry Robertson, John Gattie, and Vincent Novello.*

Smart's diary of his tour commences thus:

> August 4, Monday *Evening*
> Left Hythe at 10 m to 8 – Arrived at Dover at 20 m to 9. Mr Robertson came in the same Train (as I did from Hythe). He left London at 5 & ½ this Evening. We took a Fly from the Station to the Ship Hotel – so full there (owing to a Train not arriving in time for London for the Packets) that they got us comfortable Beds in a Private House.
>
> I was informed at the Government Packet Office that "The Princess Alice" did not go till ½ past 9 to morrow morning. When I asked at this same Office on July 31st they said this Vessel would depart at 6 in the Morning on August 5, but remarked they could not name the *exact hour* until the *day before*.
>
> Had tea with Mr Robertson at the Ship, he brought me Murray's Guide, sent by Messrs Calkin and Budd, and a French Railway Book from Mr J.Ries. I saw Mr Crevelli in the Coffee Room at the Ship, but he did not cross to Ostend with us.

| Expenses from Hythe to Bonn and back to Hythe: | £ | s | d |
|---|---|---|---|
| Brought over | 1 | 4 | 3 |
| August 4 Porter with omnibus | | | 3 |
| Omnibus from Hythe to Westenhanger Station | | 1 | 0 |
| Railway from that Station to Dover | | 3 | 6 |

The omnibus came for me at 10 m to 8 evening to Mrs Love's Lodgings
Arrived at Dover 20 m to 9 Evening.

| Fly from Station to Ship Inn ½ | | | 9 |

Mr Robertson Paid other half

August 5th

Our Luggage was brought in a Cart from the Ship Hotel to the
Vessel, Mr Robertson looked after its safe arrival on board and I
stayed on Board to watch our Places and the small Parcels. They said
'The *Princess Alice*' – Captain Smith – would sail at ½ past 9, we left
the Harbour exactly at 10 and arrived at Ostend, that is we landed –
at 20 m past 3; Excellent Passage, smooth Water and only two or
three drops of Rain – Nobody was ill. About 180 Passengers on
board (and 4 Carriages). Among these Lord Sandon, Master and
Miss Ryder, the Rev. Mr Kenaway (of Brighton), their Friend Sir
W. Magnay, late Sheriff Evans. The two latter and another Gent
were going as a Deputation on some Railway business to Brussels.
Mr and Mrs Hodgson (Brown stout) were on board, I did not see the
latter; also the Countess of Westmoreland and her little Daughter,
she had her Carriage on board in which she sat, and she travelled in
it on the Railway. She had a foreign manservant with her.

They took away our Passports as we left the Packet, which we
got again after they were stamped at the 'Bureau de Passeports'.
No charge for them, Mr Robertson assisted Lord Sandon to get his
Passport from this Office as well as to get mine.

They would not allow us to take any Baggage out of the Vessel,
but *all* was carried to the Custom house, we got it from thence after
we had dined. They only slightly searched our Baggage, they were
very civil, no charge except for taking it from the Custom House to
the R. W. Station.

After procuring our Passports we dined at ½ past 3 at the Table d'hôte at 'Hôtel de Bains', about 40 Persons dined; there had been a *previous* Dinner of, I suppose, about the same number in this Room. Plenty of Dishes – some queer ones – the Potatoes excellent, being afraid of the Vin ordinaire at 3 Franks per Bottle, I had some Brandy in addition. Two men sung, accompanying themselves on Guitars during the Dinner – not so bad – they made a collection. After dinner we got our luggage from the Custom House, they only examined it slightly – they were very civil – The Porters took it from the C. House to the R. W. Station, to which we went in good time to take our Tickets and have the luggage weighed. After that we took a walk, went into a very fine Church. I was much more pleased with Ostend than I expected.

Under the heading 'Persons I spoke to during this Tour' (ff 69v–71) Smart listed the above-mentioned in the category 'In the Vessel when crossing to Ostend'. Robertson's name is on the list too. Lord Sandon (1798-1882), heir to the Earldom of Harrowby, was M.P. for Liverpool at this time. His daughter Hon. Frances Ryder was a pupil of Smart from 1838-49. Sir William Magnay (1797-1871) was Lord Mayor of London in 1843. The Countess of Westmorland was a grand-daughter of the first Earl of Mornington (1735-81) who was a composer and Professor of Music at Trinity College, Dublin.

At Ostend Smart changed 2 Sovereigns, receiving 25.30 Francs for each (f.6).

We left Ostend at 7 – o'Clock Evening Train (we could not get ready to depart by the 4 o'Clock Train), passed through Bruges, where we stopped for 5 minutes – I got out – Lord Sandon etc. and Mr Hodgson stopped for the night at Bruges. We arrived at Ghent at 1/4 past 9 same evening. The greatest confusion in obtaining the Luggage, being dark. The Torches added to the trouble in finding it – no check as to Persons taking the wrong luggage. We left my large Carpet Bag & Robertson's Trunk at the Station for to morrow Morning and I brought my Blue Bag with me. We had a long *Walk* from the Station to the 'Hôtel de Poste' in the Place d'Armes; they could not take us in, a Commissionnaire took us another long walk to the Hôtel 'Lion d'Or', in the Place Lion d'Or, where we had Coffee, and at half-past 11 we went to a double-bedded Room (for we could not have 2 rooms), the greatest difficulty to get the Beds got ready, So, so, Room.

Owing to the Dover Train arriving *after* the Ostend Packet left Dover on Monday, the Passengers for that day joined the equally numerous Passengers on Tuesday. The Captain of the *Princess Alice* said he had never had so many as to-day and the 4 Carriages added to the crowd. One of these was Mr Hodgson's, and Lady Westmoreland sat all the voyage in the other, consequently the great quantity of Baggage caused confusion on board and also on land, and the Passengers crowded the Inns. I paid at Dover and Robertson paid all until our *arrival* at the 'Lion d'Or' Ghent, where we balanced our account up to Tuesday *night*, August 5th. I wrote to Margaret before I went to Bed.

It is little wonder that *Bradshaw's Continental Railway...Guide...for... Europe* included this advice: 'It may be adopted as one universal rule, that the less luggage a traveller embarrasses himself with, the more will he conduce to his own comfort while travelling...' It took some time for Smart to settle that day's accounts. They were detailed thus:

f.81

| | £ s d |
|---|---|
| (August) 5 | |
| Bill at Ship Inn, Dover, *My Half* | 6 9 |
| Waiter | 1 0 |
| Porter | 6 |
| Chambermaid | 1 0 |
| The Princess Alice Steam Packet | 1 1 0 |
| Steward | 1 0 |

f.8ov

| | Foreign Money Fr C |
|---|---|
| 5th August | |
| Dinner at Hotel de Bains at Table d'Hôte | 6 0 |
| ½ past 3 – Ostend | |
| Musicians in Room | 10 |
| Clear luggage & Conveying it from Custom House to Railways Station | 1 0 |

| Railway fare Ostend to Ghent | 5 0 |
| Baggage by Railway | 50 |

Settle above with Mr Robertson August 5th.

Wednesday, August 6th

As soon as I got up the Commissionnaire of the Hotel took me to the Principal Post Office, where I put in the letter to Margaret, they said I need not pay the Post.

After Breakfast of *Café au lait* the Commissionnaire of the Hotel took our *small* luggage (we left our large Luggage at the R. way Station Last Night) and walked with us to the Station. I was much pleased with the Antient Buildings in this town, particularly the Town Hall, Belfry Tower and the Church of St Bavon (a Cathedral). I was delighted with the inside of it. Seemingly a school of young ladies saying their Prayers thus early in the morning. This old town seems to be the Manchester of these Parts. Robertson paid for the Places and Baggage all the way to Cologne. We arrived before the Bureau opened, very slow in taking the Money and delivering the tickets for places. (Barriers to keep the crowd from the *payment hole*), also slow in weighing the Luggage, which when paid for and obtained the Ticket, I saw no more of it until we got to the Station at Cologne. I was allowed to take my Blue Bag inside, it was not *weighed* at *Ghent*.

I saw Lady Westmoreland & her daughter at the Ghent station, also Sir W. Magnay and his Party. I took leave of Sir W: at the *Malines* station. They went in another Train from hence to Brussels. Owing to the confusion at Malines, in changing the Carriages there, I had very nearly left my Blue Bag in the carriage we came in, which went from hence to Brussels – most fortunate in recollecting my stupidity about 2 minutes before the Brussels Train left Malines. The bustle was so great that I had no time to push among the many trying to get some of the queer looking things to eat in the Refreshment Room, therefore had nothing but my biscuits (which thanks to Margaret I brought with me) until we dined at Cologne about 11 at night. Lady Westmoreland and her daughter said they got tolerable refreshments here. I saw Mr Michaud at this station in a fuss, having been left here by the Train which took his Wife on to Brussels.[1]

The Bugles in our train sounded about ½ way between this and Liege, we soon stopped for some slight accident, which I could not make out; were not detained long. The Bugles are a better plan than our whistles (though these were used here also) because Accidents etc. could be expressed by different Bugle sounds.

The country is well described about *Liege* in Murray's Book. This Town appears to be the Birmingham of these parts, plenty of coal and (the Book says) nineteen short tunnels. The hills about here are very like Matlock.[2] It rained violently when we had left Liege about ½ an hour. Lady Westmoreland intended to sleep at Liege, she gave me a little note for Lord W, requesting me to send it to his Lodgings at Cologne, which I did by a Waiter from our Hotel the moment we arrived there, enclosing it in a Note from myself. The Messenger brought it back and said they had all gone to bed at these lodgings.

At *Verviers* we changed into Prussian Carriages. Here they would not let me take my Blue Bag into the Carriage, it was weighed & delivered to me, with my other Bag at Cologne. At Herbesthal they took our Passports, we applied for and easily obtained them at the 'Bureau de Passeports' at the Railway Station at Aix-la-Chapelle. No confusion here, they called out the Names and delivered the Passports to the owners as they answered.

Just before entering Cologne we were asked if we had anything to declare at the Customs. The Prussian Trains go faster than the Belgians and the Station Houses look better at the small Stations, but the Carriages are not so good as the Belgian ones. We ought to have left Ghent at 20 m to 9 Morning; we did not leave till 9, the Train being so long. We arrived at Cologne about 1/4 to 10 night by my Watch, but this seems to be 20 m faster here than in London. We waited in a Shed until the number of our Luggage was called out, then it was placed on a Counter before us. It was not even opened, the Officer merely asked if we had anything to declare, of course everybody said No. We delivered up our Tickets for the Baggage as

1. Noted under 'Persons I spoke to during this Tour' (see p. 37).
2. Remembered by Smart from his visit to Derbyshire in the previous summer.

the Porters took it out to the Omnibus belonging to the 'Hotel de Vienne' to which I was recommended by Mr J.Ries, arriving there about 11. We had an excellent supper of Potage and Veal Cutlets with well-dressed Potatoes. 1 Pint of Hock between us and a Glass of Brandy each. Being famished we enjoyed this meal and went to bed about 12.

A pleasant journey from Ghent: an agreeable English Lady (with her husband) who knew something of Mr Groom, at least her father did, we also talked about the Kembles and Scappa. A Polish Gent who could not speak French, made himself agreeable to Robertson, who got on famously with his German, he made all the payments to here and was most kind in saving me trouble. Nothing annoyed me but my own carelessness in nearly leaving my Blue Bag in the Carriage and having to pay for its Carriage separately at Herbesthal.

Cologne, Hotel de Vienne. Joseph Merzenich, Glockengasse, No. 6 and 8.

f. 80 v (cont.)

| | | | Fr | C |
|---|---|---|---|---|
| August 6 | | | | |
| Wednesday | I paid at Herbesthal for weighing my *Blue Bag* only which they would not let me take inside the Carriage | | | |
| | | *I believe* | | 19 |
| August 6 | Hotel de Lion d'Or Ghent | | 6 | 50 |
| | Commission at Ghent | | 1 | 0 |
| | Railway to Herbesthal (from Ghent) | | 3 | 0 |
| | from ditto to Cologne | | 9 | 50 |
| | Baggage | | 2 | 17 |

It is hoped that the pollution problem in Cologne was less acute than when Coleridge wrote in 1834 how he

> ...*counted two and seventy stenches,*
> *All well defined, and several stinks!*
> *Ye Nymphs that reign o'er sewers and sinks,*
> *The river Rhine, it is well known,*
> *Doth wash your city of Cologne;*
> *But tell me, Nymphs, what power divine*
> *Shall henceforth wash the river Rhine.*

# CHAPTER 5

# Preparations in Bonn

In 1560 work on the Cathedral in Cologne came to an end. The choir was complete, but of the rest the nave existed only as a series of pillars taken up to the height of the capitals and the aisles were un-vaulted. For centuries the choir served as cathedral and the unfinished parts of the work lay separate and forlorn. In Napoleonic times the city lost its diocesan status and its Archbishop. Soon after the liberation of Germany, however, there was a call for the restoration and completion of the cathedral as being a national monument. Among those who led the movement for the final realisation of the great medieval concept were Joseph Gorres and Goethe. In 1821 the Archdiocese was re-established and soon afterwards Schinkel's pupil F. A. Ahlert began work on the project of completion. In 1841 a *Zentral-Dombau-Verein* was established to further the enterprise and in the next year the King of Prussia laid the foundation stone of the new work. After Ahlert's death the architects in charge of operations were E. F. Zwirner and R. Voigtel. Although work was not finally completed until 1880 it was possible to consecrate the whole building in 1848. Two years later the cathedral was memorialized by Robert Schumann in the fourth movement of his 'Rhenish' Symphony.

Thursday, August 7th
Settled Accounts (at Breakfast) with Mr Robertson up to this
Morning. I got up with a Headache (at $\frac{1}{2}$ past 5) thanks to Margaret
for the Soda she gave me I did not suffer long – I suppose eating &

drinking so late gave me the usual Cramp which I was rather free
from the Night before; After Breakfast – walked with Robertson to
see the Cathedral (Murray page 247). The interior most beautiful.
They were at Prayers in the Choir (no Organ or Singing). A few
men were at work outside but there has been much built since I was
here with C. Kemble in 1825 [see p. 11].

The *Pole* who travelled with us yesterday seemed glad to meet us
at the Cathedral. We had little time to spare, therefore we rather
hurried back to our Hotel, losing our way thither. We found a
One Horse Wheeled Carriage at the door ready to convey us to the
Bonn Railway Station. We had understood that it was to have been
an Omnibus. The Station Room is beautiful, charmingly situated
near the Town Walls. Pleased with some Engravings round the Room
these being views of some of the Towns etc. we came through.

Left Cologne about 20 m past 10 – arrived Bonn at $\frac{1}{2}$ past 11 –
The first thing we saw was an Omnibus waiting from 'The Hotel de
Trêves'. The Commissionnaire of this Hotel, alias the Conductor of
the Omnibus, to whom we gave the Tickets for the Luggage,
procured it for us and placed it on the top of the Omnibus. It appears
that each first-rate Hotel sends its own Omnibus to the Station, an
excellent plan to get Customers, some of these Carriages are very
fine.

In its time, because of its situation, Bonn had suffered many vicissitudes.
In the seventeenth century it was besieged by Austrians and Spaniards,
and also by Friedrich III, Elector of Brandenburg. During the War of
Spanish Succession it was occupied by the British under Marlborough
and during the Napoleonic Wars suffered the indignity of being transferred to French dominion. Rescued from this in 1813, Bonn then
became part of the far-flung territories of the Kingdom of Prussia.

For thirty years since that time Bonn had settled down to its reduced
status of a tourist centre and grown accustomed to invasion by English
milords. On Sunday mornings an English Church Service was held
in the former Electoral Chapel. Visitors to the city were shown two
houses of special interest. The one was Bonngasse Nr. 515, where
Beethoven was born, the other Rheingasse Nr. 934, where he spent

most of his boyhood. In 1845 the former property (now the Beethoven House) belonged to a Dr Schild and the latter to a master-baker named Fischer.[1]

Simrock, landlord of the Hotel de Trêves, was brother of Peter Joseph Simrock, the music publisher. Their father, Nikolaus Simrock (1752-1834) had been a horn player in the Electoral orchestra before becoming a music-publisher. From 1805 the elder Simrock was undertaking the publication of works by Beethoven.

> Politely received by Simrock at his 'Hôtel de Trèves', Bonn, but the Rooms Jo:Ries engaged for us were then occupied, not well arranged, as we arrived on the day stipulated; however we dressed in a very good Chambre and our Clothes were removed at Night to the Rooms Simrock gave us (on the 2nd Floor) instead of those we were to have had on the 3rd. I was pleased with his explanation about his intended charges. We shall see.
>
> Dined at the table-d'hôte at $\frac{1}{2}$ past 1 (the stated hour was 1 but nothing is exact here except the Railways and they are only tolerably so). Plenty of Dishes, some good. Our Pole, who travelled with us, dined here tho' he said he should stay in Cologne to see the sights. I left the Dinner table to write to Margaret; Robertson and I took it to the Post, which is in the same place as, at that time, Beethoven's *covered* Statue was.

The statue stood in the Münsterplatz where formerly there had been a fine medieval Penitents' Cross. Under the shadow of the great church the Place, fragrant with the scent of its lime trees, was beautiful.

> Then we went to the 1st General Rehearsal in the Riding School, which is well fitted up for the purpose. It was to have begun at 3, it did about 4. The pieces rehearsed were Beethoven's Mass in D, conducted by Spohr, and a new cantata, by Liszt, conducted (with plenty of twisting of the person), by himself.
>
> As a whole the Mass is too difficult in many parts – to me – non-effective. The Chorus singers most excellent, the Band, good particularly the Strings. The Trumpets are not so well toned as ours.

1. *Die Universitätsstadt Bonn und ihre Umgebungen*, 2nd ed., Bonn, 1851, p.23.

I missed the organ for which there is a part in the score, which
Mr Flowers,[2] my Pupil and Friend, lent me to look over. The
Principal Singers: *Canto*, Mlle Tuczek[3] hurried too much. I suppose
she was nervous. Alto, Mlle Schloss,[4] who was in London, very good,
but was frequently like the Canto, too *forte*. Tenor, Herr Beyer[5] –
so so. Bass, Staudigl,[6] excellent. On account of the Principal Singers,
particularly the 1st canto, many passages were repeated, several
times, the choruses doubtless had had many rehearsals, superintended,
as I understood by Weber of Cologne.

After the Mass, Liszt's Cantata was rehearsed, for which we stayed
till about the few last Bars, when we heard (as we were leaving the
yard) the Trumpet and Drums saluting Liszt at the end of his
Cantata, as they did Spohr just *before* the Mass began. They both
conducted from a tall closed up Pulpit, the Conductor's *back* to the
*Secondo* side, bad plan this. It was nearly dark when Liszt's Cantata
ended.

Persons I saw at Rehearsal – Spohr & his Wife, he took us into the
Gallery that we might hear better. He came up there during Liszt's
Cantata, he went away after 2 thirds of it, being tired with
conducting and so hot that he had his wife's Shawl put on over his
Great Coat. He does not seem very strong. I understood that a new
opera of his has succeeded lately [see p. 27].

I also spoke to Liszt, Staudigl, Mlle Schloss, to whom I was
introduced by her desire by Mr Geo: French Flowers, who made
himself and Pupil (a rich man he said Mr Athanasious Diedrick
*Wackerberth*) known to me. As I could not make out his name I got
him to write it on his Card. Mr F. said he is to give an *impartial*
account of this Festival for three Papers. The fine things he said about
my conducting were rather too much for even Germany.

2. George French Flowers, organist, and music critic of the *Literary Gazette*.
3. Leopoldine Tuczek (1821-83), Bohemian singer employed in Berlin.
4. A singer from Cologne.
5. Also a singer from Cologne.
6. Joseph Staudigl (1807-61) sang in the Kärntnertor Theatre in Vienna, was a famous
oratorio and Lieder singer, and gave a memorable interpretation of the title role in
Mendelssohn's *Elijah* at its first performance in Birmingham in 1846.

Mr and Mrs Oury[7] accompanied by Mr Gardiner[8] (Mail) were
there. After the rehearsal left my Card at Dr Breidenstein's house
with the maidservant as he was out; had it not rained we would have
gone to seek him at the Town Hall or the Casino. She said he would
be either at the one or other – returned to Hotel, had Coffee for
Supper and went to Bed early.

Thank God that we made the Journey Safely to Bonn.

Before going to bed, however, the day's accounts were recorded.

f. 80

Prussian money Tl S g

August 7
'Hotel de Vienne' Cologne. Bill for Bed and Breakfast

|  | | |
|---|---|---|
| | I | 14 |
| Paid Robertson £1.11 at Hotel de Vienne, Cologne, which includes Bill at that Hotel and *From* August 6 over leaf | 5 | |
| Repaid Mr Robertson for Ticket he paid to 1st Rehearsal at ½ past 4 Thursday this Afternoon | | 15 |
| & for Postage of a letter to Margaret | | 7 |
| he gave me ½ a Groschen back | | |
| therefore the Postage of a letter is 6½ Groschen | | |
| Repaid Mr Robertson for omnibus to Bonn Railway | | 5 |
| Railway to Bonn *from Cologne* | | 15 |
| luggage to Bonn | | 1 |

Brought up

The day had been an anxious one for Breidenstein. First, the concert hall
that had been specially built for this Festival was not yet finished and the

7. Antonio James Oury (1800-83), son of an Italian father and English mother, was a
violinist who led the orchestra of the King's Theatre, London. His wife, née Anna
Caroline de Belleville, a native of Bavaria, was a pianist. She had studied with Czerny
in Vienna from 1816-20, during which time she had met Beethoven on a number of
occasions. They were accompanied by their adopted son Sivori. Mrs Oury's father
joined them in Bonn.
8. William Gardiner (1770-1853), a Leicester hosiery manufacturer, was an enthusiastic
and well informed musical amateur. He was an early admirer of Haydn and Beethoven,
to whom there are many references in his *Music and Friends* (I and II, 1838, III 1853). (See
p. 8).

*L. van Beethoven*

*Birthplace of Beethoven*

Cologne from the West bank of the Rhine in 1846

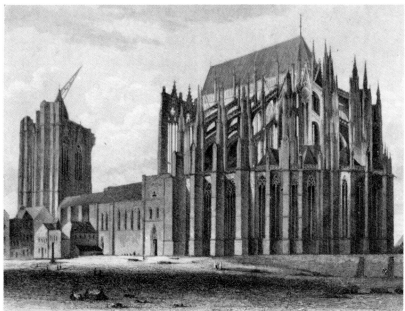

The cathedral at Cologne in 1846

*View of Bonn in 1846*

*The cathedral at Bonn in 1846*

*Louis Spohr*

*Concert in the Beethoven Hall during the Festival*

Domenico Dragonetti

Franz Liszt

*Godesberg*

*The Convent at Nonnenwerth and the ruins of Rolandseek*

Queen Victoria and Prince Albert enter Cologne

*The Royal Yacht passes the Drachenfels*

*The Queen and the Prince arrive by Royal Train at Brühl*

*The Queen passes Coblenz*

*Details of bas-reliefs on Beethoven Monument*

DIE FANTASIE

DIE SYMPHONIE

DIE GEISTLICHE MUSIK

DIE DRAMATISCHE MUSIK

rehearsals had to be held in the Riding School. Then most of the partici-
pants were staying in Cologne, from where they would commute with
Bonn. But the exigencies of train time-tables made it necessary to keep
an eye on the timing of rehearsals. On the first day of combined
rehearsal there were two; by the beginning of the next week there were
six or seven of one sort or another each day. Breidenstein thought with
Smart that Liszt's conducting left something to be desired. He felt that
the performers were happier with Spohr's quieter but more secure
methods.

August 8, Friday
Breakfasted at 8 and then Table d'Hôte at one, as on former days.
Received a letter from Margaret at 1/4 past nine, dated August 5th.
   There was a Rehearsal *this morning* of *parts* of Beethoven's Mass in D
and Choral Sinfonia. We did not go to this Rehearsal, but walked
about the town until severe Rain drove us home, there were one or
two claps of Thunder this morning:—
   In the Afternoon we went to a Rehearsal in the Minster, (it began
about ½ past 4) of Beethoven's Mass in C. Nothing else rehearsed.
The band & Chorus were *behind* the high Altar, out of sight to us in
a Pew about the middle of the Church, which was prettily decorated
with Flowers and Green Garlands. The four principal singers *sounded*
to be the same as at the Rehearsal last night. The Chorus was strong
and good. All the Principal singers sung well. They said the Tenor
was an amateur, I doubt that, but his voice was not strong enough.
The Band was good, the Wind Instruments played excellently, but
the Band was not strong enough for the Voices (I suppose there was
not room for a larger Band). Dr Breidenstein conducted, we could
not see him. I do not agree as to the time taken for some of the
movements, they were generally too slow and in the 'Benedictus'
too fast. Many parts of this beautiful Mass were unsteady, the fault
seemed to be with the worthy Conductor who may not have had
sufficient experience, besides this there was a small Echo in the part
where the Band was placed. Mr and Mrs Spohr came in about the
middle of the Mass, he left his seat to go up into the Orchestra,
probably to speak to the conductor about the wrong times. Mr

Robertson saw Oury, Gardiner, Flowers and his friend *Waekerbarth*, Flowers says he is an Englishman, (he is Professor, somewhere in England, of Anglo-Saxon). The two latter joined us after coming out of the Church as we were looking at some Foot Soldiers in the place where Beethoven's Statue is. They were waiting for the King of Prussia's arrival, which we went to see at the Bonn Railroad Terminous.

The King and Queen[9] in one carriage came from Cologne, at Bonn the carriage was taken off the Truck. 6 Post Horses put to it at the Station – Ropes to leaders for Traces. They passed us at a quick pace, no other Soldiers but 2 first to clear the way, tho' there were some at the Station. 3 or 4 other Carriages, one of them Royal, post horses to them also. I believe the party went to Stolzenfels.

The King's arrival made Bonn all alive, they talked of Fireworks to be at Coblentz in honor of our Queen, the finest that ever have been.

Went to the 'Golden Star', near our hotel in the marketplace, to visit Liszt; he had not returned from meeting the King at Cologne about the arrangements. We then intended to visit Spohr (in the same Hotel) we met him and Mrs S. coming downstairs. We went with them to the large Music Hall (to be described). On our way back we left my card with Dr Breidenstein's man Servant, who was standing at the Door. The Doctor was out and we explained that I left a Card for him with the *Maid* servant last night. We next called again on Liszt, also at the 'Golden Star', he was then out of Town; Handel Gear[10] was standing at the Door of the Hotel, has taken rooms out of it for six Thalers a night during the days of the Festival.

When leaving this hotel Mr Fétis[11] of Brussels made himself known to me (Mrs F. was with him). I suppose he remembered me

9. Friedrich Wilhelm IV of Prussia. He had married Princess Elisabeth of Bavaria.
10. Henry Handel Gear (1805-84), sometime chorister of Chapel Royal and St Paul's Cathedral, was organist of Grace Church, New York City (Broadway at 10th Street), from 1882–8. After studying singing on the continent he settled in London where he was active as singer, teacher, and organist.
11. François Joseph Fétis (1784-1871), Belgian scholar and Director of the Brussels Conservatoire.

in London. I gave him my Bonn Card. Mr Flowers said that Mr Davison[12] of the *Musical World* is to arrive.

We went to call this Evening upon Mr Simrock (Brother of our Landlord) at his Music Shop. The maid servant at first said he was at home and I gave her my Card but she returned saying he was out. I think not true – never mind – a Bore saved – Returned home to Coffee and went to Bed 1/4 before 10 – Saturday August 9th – After a walk in the town, (as we did not wish to hear the rehearsals in the Fest-halle,) and buying tickets from our Landlord, Simrock, for all the performances and Dr Breidenstein's account of the Festival[13] (2s English) we went to Godesberg in the Omnibus from the Railway Station at 20 m past 11. This Omnibus waits at the Station to take the Passengers to Godesberg who may come from Cologne; we got there in an hour. We dined at the Table d'hôte at 20 m past 1 at the Grand Hôtel de Belle-vue. The Father of an English Family (that is of 2 ignorant tall Sons) had met me at Dr Carnaby's – *they* travelled in the 2nd class, and his Wife, pleasant woman, an invalid, with us in the first class. (Bad music during the Dinner, they play in an adjoining room as it rained). Notwithstanding the Rain we walk to the Castle at Godesberg. The view charming from the top, which we ascended by a tolerable Staircase, which the King of Prussia is coming to look at tomorrow, in case our Queen should like to ascend. She is to reside at Brühl and Stolzenfels – Castles belonging to the King of Prussia, the 1st between Bonn & Cologne, the second between Godesberg and Mayence. The Landlady of the Hotel, a sharp woman, was loud in her praise of Prince Albert, who, she said, had often dined and brought parties into the Room we dined in. Had we been Germans this amiable Lady would doubtless have been equally loud in the praise of some German Prince who had dined there also. The Scholars in the university at Bonn (I suppose *Princes* are the exception) are not allowed to come so far as Godesberg, the landlady said *feelingly*, for fear they should spend too much, besides it might lead to Gambling.

12. James William Davison (1813-85), the music critic of *Saturday Review* and *Pall Mall Gazette*, and of *The Times* from 1846-79.
13. *Festgabe zu der am 12ten August 1845 stattfindenden Inauguration des Beethoven-Monuments.*

Returned to Bonn at 10 m past 4 in the same Omnibus we came in and with us our Landlady with plenty of empty baskets, doubtless to bring back full for her Guests. It seems that she met the English Family who dined with us, as she was coming from Cologne (by Railway) and strongly recommended *her own* Hotel at Godesberg as those at Bonn would be so dear/so they closed with her and mean to come into Bonn for the performances and return after them.

When we came back we walked to the Terrace or Altezoll where there is a beautiful view of the Rhine, the Drachenfels & 7 Mountains, the Castle at Godesberg, the Bridge of 9 Boats, (the Ferry from Bonn to the opposite Shore) is clever – the Boats are made fast to each other at some distance between each, a Rope made fast in the Ground passes over each Boat to the ferry Boat (2 Boats together with a sort of Gallows on them to which the Rope is fixed) then by the management of the Helm, as the Ferry Boat cannot go down it is driven across by the Current. On our return to the Hotel I found cards from Messrs Hodgson and Hogarth,[14] stuck in my Key, No. 16 – a good plan.

I went to the Golden Stern Hotel, Chambre No. 37, to visit Mr Hogarth, he came with me to Simrock's Hotel. The following also came into our Coffee Room, Messrs Gruneison,[15] Barnet[16] (Post), Kenney[17] came with Davison, Wild Jun., Handel Gear and some Gent said that Lord and Lady Westmoreland were at the Rehearsal this morning for a short time and also that they looked in during the Table d'hôte at the Golden Stern, and that his Lordship particularly desired to be remembered to me. They were on their way to visit the King of Prussia. It seems that all our musical Great Guns are at the Golden Star, about 120 dined at the Table d'Hôte. *They* said I ought to have been there. *I* say I am more quiet – (tho' noisy

14. George Hogarth (1783-1870), father-in-law of Charles Dickens was a musical historian, composer, and music critic on this occasion for the *Morning Chronicle*.
15. Charles Lewis Gruneisen (1806-79), a journalist, was representing the *Illustrated News* and *Britannia* at Bonn.
16. Morris Barnett (1800-56), an actor at Drury Lane, was also a music critic, sent to the Beethoven Festival by the *Morning Post*.
17. Charles Lamb Kenney (1821-81) godson of Charles Lamb and a clerk in the General Post Office and a recognised wit, represented *The Times*.

enough) – at the Hôtel de Trèves. Mr Barnet lives at our Hotel.

We left Bonn under an Arch of the University College (on the left of the *inside* of this Gate is the way thro' a Garden, to the beautiful view of the Terrace). The Hotels and Houses are on the left, at the commencement of the Road, are large and well situated, fronting the walks, belonging to the College, which are well shaded by the tall Trees. The backs of these Hotels and Houses look to the Rhine, they must be very pleasant and not too far from any part of Bonn. The Road to Godesberg is straight and very good, only paved in part here and there in a Village. The Country is highly cultivated, no Hedges but plenty of Vines – they look like, but not so well as, our Hop Grounds – we could not see the Rhine till we were at Godesberg, near to which, on the left hand, going thither, is a Cross by the side of the Road. Our talkative Landlady said it had been erected by one Brother who had killed another (but see Murray, page 264). The View from the Hotel door was very fine.

The expenses of the day amounted to:

f. 79v.

| August 9 – Godesberg | 5 | |
| Omnibus to *Godesberg* | 5 | |
| ditto from | | |
| Table d'Hôte at Godesberg | 1 0 | |

While Smart and other of his companions were disporting themselves at Godesberg, Breidenstein was continuing to discover fresh difficulties. During Saturday afternoon, the only time the cathedral was available for rehearsing this work, he went through the Mass in C. Afterwards, having borrowed the music room in the University he took some of his choir through his own work. Not all the singers, however, turned up; presumably, thought Breidenstein, because they had not been informed as to what room they should attend.

# CHAPTER 6

# Opening Ceremonies

On Sunday the city of Bonn assumed her festival apparel. Most of the householders decorated their properties, and the flags of Bonn, of Prussia, of Bavaria, and of England (in honour of Queen Victoria and Prince Albert who were to arrive next day), hung from many windows. The statue in the Münsterplatz was veiled, but already around its base were wreaths and more flags. The University opened its collections to general view, and visitors thronged the Aula, with its descriptive and decorative frescoes, the rooms devoted respectively to Rhineland history and antiquities, and the natural history displays at Poppelsdorf. As the morning wore on those who were in holiday mood wandered into the gardens by the river, where, engaged by the Beethoven Committee, two bands discoursed agreeable music.

> Sunday, August 10
> Went with Messrs Gruneisen, Hogarth & Robertson to hear part of Mass in the Minster Church – then with Robertson to look at the Jesuits' fine Church; an energetic Priest, in a White Sermon [sic] was preaching extemporaneously. Robertson could not understand his German. We could not see the organ (if there is one) as we did not like to move from under the Gallery at the entrance; the organ in the Minster is coarse and out of tune. Men only were chanting the Mass, no band there. Before dinner, by Gruneisen's desire, I took to his Room, in the Golden Star, a copy of Dr Breidenstein's letter of invitation to me.

We had about 100 at our Table d'Hôte today at one o'Clock and apparently there were as many dishes (about 300 – *they said* dined at the Table d'Hôte at the Golden Star.) I went into Mr and Mrs Oury's *Bed* Room (2 Beds) at that Hotel to see a M.S. Copy belonging to Oury of a Cantata by Beethoven's which Oury doubts if he will give it to the King of Prussia or to Prince Albert. *Doubtless* he will fix on the latter. Mr Fétis came into the Room brought by Mr Gardiner. Mrs Oury's Father was also introduced to me here.

At the Goldener Stern the landlord, Herr Schmidt, had shown great enterprise and built a supplementary dining-room for the Festival. Capable of accommodating 500 diners the room was happily named the Beethoven Room. The company at the Table d'Hôte on the first day was a brilliant one indeed. Those present included Liszt, the Spohrs, Berlioz, the Schumanns, Moscheles, Charles Halle, Johannes Verhulst – Schumann's former pupil from Holland, Meyerbeer, Wolf – the poet who had provided the words for Liszt's cantata, Viardot-Garcia, Jenny Lind, Anton Schindler, and most of the press. Champagne – not, complained Davison, of the best quality – was liberally dispensed. At the end of the room was a portrait of Beethoven. Above the portrait was a gallery. In the gallery a quadrille band played waltzes and operatic selections throughout the proceedings.

After our Table d'Hôte Robertson and I went to Review of a Regiment of Cavalry by the King of Prussia in the long walk near the Railway Station. The King came on horseback with a numerous staff – the Queen in a Carriage and there were other Carriages in the suite. It was a fine sight, but the Rain took away the pleasure of looking at it. The Brass Band of the Regiment had a fine effect, but the *mob* was too obligato and the trotting about of the Soldiers to keep us back was troublesome. This Royal inspection was soon over and the King departed as he came, with cheers, but not very hearty ones.

I forgot to mention that we went this morning, at $\frac{1}{2}$ past 10 to the Rehearsal of Liszt's Cantata in the Great Hall. I left Robertson there

while I called upon Mr Hodgson at a capital Hotel as to the view of
the Rhine from the back, called Hôtel Belle Vue. I knocked at, and
was let into, Mrs Hodgson's *Bedroom* by herself and maid, from
thence we went into a capital Sitting Room. The Cook is so famous
at this hotel that *She* is employed very much *out* of it, therefore the
eating is so bad that Mr and Mrs Hodgson dine at the Golden Star –
where it seems that everybody (fond of a crowd) dine [*sic*]. Mr H.
kindly invited me and Mr Robertson to drink Tea with him this
Evening to hear the music and see the Fireworks from his Hotel, we
were too tired after the Concert to go, besides it rained.

After coming from the inspection of the Regiment we called upon
Mr Ries. He is a very fine, agreeable old man and upwards of
ninety.[1] He seemed to enjoy our conversation. He had been to one
Rehearsal, too infirm to go to the concerts – said that Beethoven's
Grand Father was a Chapel Master, but his Father was only a Tenor
Chorus Singer, and so little was thought of young Beethoven that
no one can say in which house in Bonn he was born, tho' 2 houses
claim that honor, but what is more extraordinary, old Mr Ries said,
tho' it was known that Beethoven died in Vienna, no one could say
*where* he was *buried*.[2] I was charmed with my visit and promised to
repeat it.

At 1/4 past 5 (doors opened at 5) we went to the 1st Concert. It
was announced to begin at 6 – See Bill No. 1. According to the
inscription over the Entrance Door, which was brought past our
Hotel by the workmen in procession singing, this hall was built in a
short time. (Translated by Mr Robertson).

'Through the union and enthusiasm of the Citizens of Bonn
erected in 11 Days, from the 27th of July to the 7th of August 1845.'

The New Fest Hall therefore was built in this short time, Mr
Zwiner [*sic*], Architect of the Cathedral at Cologne, planned this

1. Franz Anton Ries (1755-1846), father of Ferdinand, had been a pupil of Salomon and
one of Beethoven's teachers. He had befriended the Beethoven family after the death of
the mother and in their extreme poverty. After 1794, unlike most other court musicians,
Ries remained in Bonn where he held various civic offices. He had a house in Godesberg.
In 1845 he was given an honorary Doctorate (see p.88) and the Order of the Red Eagle.
2. See pp. 76 and 92.

Hall which is

200 F. Long

75 F. Broad

36 F. High in the Center

20 F. ditto at the sides

They say it will hold 4000 Persons, so it may with the Orchestra and Standing Room (over the Door outside are Flags, on the largest of which is (translated) 'Union makes Strength'.)

The following description is taken when looking to the orchestra, which was much too low, and the platform did not rise sufficiently, indeed it was more of a slope than rising. All the Chorus were in the front, bad for the Band could not penetrate thro' them being too low & too far back. The Conductor was in a handsome Pulpit, his desk was placed to face the Primo Side. The Leader was not situated as at the Philh. but nearly according to our former plan, not elevated. The 4 Principal Singers were on the *Secondo* Side, much elevated, rather behind the Conductor who had to turn round to them and to turn to the *Secondo* side when necessary. The Principal Singers should have been on the Primo Side and the Conductor should have been a little in advance with his back to the Public.

A large space – and 6 Benches all across – was railed off in front of the Orchestra, I suppose for the Royal Party and officials to-morrow night. (It is curious that in the Tablets round the room relative to Beethoven the one close to where we sat was the Mount of Olives – and the one over the Royal Box was appropriately...'The Battle of Victoria'.)[3] Mr Robertson made a drawing of the Room and doubtless we shall have it in the *illustrated News* – a bad plan to enter immediately from the Street with no Ante Room for the departure of the Audience. 2 doors at the bottom of the Room were opened, but the flight of steps at the entrance would be most dangerous if there was a rush from behind. The Performers entered from another Street, thro' a 'Restoration' Room (a passage for them in it railed off). The Carte for the Wines etc. seemed dear. Opposite the door (on the right) of this Room were two other doors, the one near the Orchestra to admit into the reserve place. I thought the lighting of the

3. See p. 57.

Room by a few Chandeliers and many containing many
Candles made it brilliant enough – tolerably well ventilated by rows
of opened Windows on each side of the Hall – none of the Benches
covered – but sufficiently wide and far apart – the regulations for the
seats were well managed and might be made perfect; the sides of
Benches were numbered thus – [*see opposite*]

   To those who bought Tickets for the 3 Concerts a *White* Card
was given with the number of the Bench on it which you are to go
to, ours was No. 18. You could take any unoccupied seat on *this
bench* (better if they had been *numbered*, if a sufficient quantity of
Servants to keep them, and easy access could be made to them).
You keep this *White* Card, giving up the others per Concert, and go
to the *same Bench* for each, when those who arrive the soonest get the
seat they choose *on this Bench*, but it is difficult to prevent intruders
on the Bench, for Mr Gladstone[4] not being aware of this regulation,
bought a Ticket for *one* Concert, this did not give him the right to a
seat on a reserved Bench, therefore he was stopped in going to one,
but seeing me, he said, he made his way up the side to the Bench
behind me. The men stood in the middle Aisle to prevent our going
*Higher* than the Bench numbered on your White Card. Mr Magrath
came here from Dublin, he is at our Hotel.

Davison adds a critical, slightly cynical, note to this, observing that 'as
[the building] took no more than eleven days in building, any striking
beauty of design or ornament was hardly to be expected...At the
furthermost end of the room, on the right hand side, two doors open
into a refreshment room, where cakes, and wines, and sandwiches and
seltzer water, and cigars, etc. may be procured during the performances:
as these, however, and especially the cigars, must be consumed on the
premises – though as the doors are always open, any body not as smoke-
dried as a German, will be sensible of a pleasant odour of tobacco,
during the greater part of whatever entertainment he may chance to
attend in the Beethoven Hall. At the furthermost end of the room is a
very equivocal portrait of Beethoven, "in doubtful oil", at either side

4. William Ewart Gladstone (1809-98), M.P. for Newark, who had just resigned office as
President of the Board of Trade.

and might be made perfectly the
Sides of Benches were numbered
thus

*Orchestra*  Platform for
P. Waltz and
Principal Singers.

Royal Box

Door.   *Reserved Places* — letter A

Refuge to
available

1
2
3
4
&c

Door
to
Refreshmt
Room

Difficult to show the Reserved line
Passage for leading
...
Door

Means of entry Rejected in this
Passage below the numbers of your Wakefield

Not reserved
Benches

Reserved line

Reserved
Benches

Difficult to show the
Reserved line
Passage for standing

Shown    Entrance    Exit

57

of which are two figures, supported by two angels, who are placing a wreath on the brow of the great composer, while he is writing the Mass in D'.

The opening concert began at 6 o'clock in the evening.

> The Mass in D is too complicated in parts but was well performed, particularly by the Chorus & Band, and well conducted, so was the Sinfonia The Ode to Joy, which went famously. The P's & F's so well attended to that I never heard this Sinfonia so well performed before, but the Trumpets had a bad tone. The Drums *beat* our Chipp[5] much better in time; the

> was capital, the Oboe & Bassoon better than ours, the latter only as to tone, the Horns much better played than ours, yet the whole effect is not sufficiently loud. The Chorus too strong for the voices, the Principal Singers in this Ode infinitely more effective than ours, but the German words seem to suit better (I was delighted to see how orderly the Performers were in obeying the Conductor.)
>
> The Audience was most attentive. Great applause to Spohr when the Band saluted him with Drums & Trumpets as I have before described. In order to make silence before the *Sinfonia* began there was a short roll of the Drum – good idea, as it made the audience sit down in expectation of the commencement. They were noisy when some of the Company stood up. Upon the whole arrangements were excellent inside and out, with the Police keeping the ranks. Notwithstanding this so-called excellent police, Mr Wild[6] Jun., of our

5. Thomas Paul Chipp (1793-1870), harpist and drummer in London orchestras.
6. Henry Wylde (1822-90), former student of R.A.M. of which he became a professor, organist, and conductor.

Hotel, had his Pocket picked of his Passport etc; fortunately there were only memoranda in his Pocket Book. They said that one of the many Pickpockets was taken – I hope not an *English* Professor of that art.

A large party at supper at our hotel, among them Blasis, the Clarionet player and his agreeable wife, Madame Meerti, both living at our Hotel.[7] Blasis was at the Rehearsal this morning. Mr M. Barnett supped with us and his Morning Herald friend, Mr Feemy or Famy. We had Coffee only for our Supper.

The Inauguration intended for tomorrow postponed until Tuesday by Royal command – this puts off the Concert one day.

The soloists in the Mass were Tuczek, Schloss, Beier, and Staudigl, while Hartmann of Cologne was the violin soloist in the 'Benedictus'. For the Symphony the two first-named were replaced by Fräulein Sachs from Cologne and Fräulein Kratky from Frankfurt. Beier was not in good form. He was unwell, and he had only been instructed to take over the tenor part in the Symphony, due to there having been no answer from either Joseph Tichatscheck of Dresden or Götz, on the day before the general rehearsal. The audience for the first concert numbered 1800.

The performances were treated somewhat unkindly by some of the critics – Davison included – and later that night a variety of opinion was expressed round the tables in the Goldener Stern. The Committee was pulled to pieces, and so was Liszt whose enemies were numerous and vocal, Breidenstein noted, however, the enthusiastic responses of Ludwig Rellstab, the critic of the *Vossische Zeitung*, Fétis (though Fétis told Davison he thought the last movement of the Choral Symphony 'detestable'), and Berlioz.

Those with reserves of energy went to see a firework display on the Rhine. Smart, it would seem, went to his room to write a letter to Margaret.

Meanwhile, the British Royal Yacht, with Queen Victoria and Prince Albert aboard, was lying at anchor off Antwerp.

7. Arnold Joseph Blaes (1814-92), virtuoso clarinettist and professor in the Brussels Conservatoire. His wife Elisa (née Meerti) was a soprano singer of repute.

# CHAPTER 7

# The Good Ship 'Ludwig van Beethoven'

Right from the moment when he was coopted on to the Beethoven Committee Liszt had been a cause of dissension. From the point of view of the Bonn members Liszt was avid for publicity for himself, opinionated and – so far as public money was concerned – extravagant. He, on the other hand, found the Germans exceedingly dull and entirely lacking in knowing how a great event should be arranged and carried out. Breidenstein was badly cast as the villain of a piece, or as the General Secretary of an ambitious undertaking. A musicologist, he had only taken over the full secretarial duties a few months before the Festival on the death of Schlegel. Having done so he committed a series of gaffes.

Moscheles, for instance, was invited to take part in the Festival, but only to accompany Fräulein Kratky in the performance of *Adelaide*. Moscheles, one of the more celebrated pianists of the day, was not pleased. He declined the invitation, which in any case was a belated one. Then there was the matter of the press. Breidenstein wondered why the foreign press should have free tickets for the concerts, and having wondered he then refused to supply them. Ashamed at such disregard for the proper conventions Liszt bought tickets for those journalists who were without them, and paid for them out of his own pocket. The English journalists, however, had paid for their own.

On the morning of 11 August Smart woke up with a sense of grievance. He had informed Breidenstein of his intention to come to Bonn well in advance of the Festival, but so far Breidenstein had taken no notice of him. Smart was conscious of the respect due to the Composer

of Her Britannic Majesty's Chapel Royal, and wrote a letter to Breidenstein. He kept a copy (ff. 73–2).

> Hotel de Trèves
> Bonn
> Monday August 11th 1845

Sir,

  I shall be much obliged by you acquainting the Committee that I
arrived in Bonn on *Thursday* last according to the invitation they
honored me with to be present at the 'Inauguration of the statue',
which ceremony is to take place *tomorrow morning*; Mr Jos:Ries has
informed me that he delivered to you my reply to the letter you
favored me with, in which I mentioned that I hope to be allowed to
pay my respects to you, I called *twice* at your house for that purpose,
but was informed you were not at home, I conclude that your
Servants have not delivered the Card I left upon each of my visits
with my address *here* written on it, therefore I have been deprived of
the pleasure I had anticipated;—

> I have the honor to be
> Sir
> your obedient Servt.
> G. S.

One of the Conductors of the Concert given in London on July 19th
1837 in aid of the fund for the Beethoven Monument.

  To Dr Breidenstein President of the Committee etc etc etc

Early that morning Breidenstein had a full-scale rehearsal, and then he
considered what to do about his dereliction of duty. In this he was
helped by Liszt, who remembered Smart's kindness to him, years
before, when as a boy of thirteen he had paid his first visit to England.

Monday, August 11th
Took letter to Post for Margaret & left letter for Dr Breidenstein
(See Copy in the Book – at the other end after Account of Expences).
Called on Mme Spohr, her Husband was at rehearsal. On my return
to our Hotel I found Moscheles (who had previously called upon me)
with Dr Breidenstein, the latter had been to leave Tickets for me at
our Hotel. The Dr B. made the amende honorable for all his former
neglect. He stated, probably the fact, that his head was turned with

the quantity he had to attend to. Greatly concerned that I should have had such just cause for complaint. He gave me a ticket (and also one for Robertson) to admit to *every Sight* and place and invited us to walk in the Procession tomorrow morning to the Minster and Inauguration. Next came Liszt with his apologies for the neglect of the Committee. He could never intend a slight *to me*. It seems that my letter to Dr Breidenstein wrought these wonderful attentions from the Committee. I readily pardoned their neglect, knowing how I have been occupied upon similar occasions, but query, will the *Press* pardon their not having had Tickets *given* to them?

Then Dr Breidenstein invited us to the Christening and trip in the Steam Ship 'Beethoven' to which the General Pass Tickets, which we received this Morning from him, would admit.

We went with Moscheles in an Omnibus from the Golden Star, (Gratis) to the place where the Cologne Steam Boats land their Passengers near the Ferry. In getting on board the *Beethoven* we had nearly been either crushed to death or pushed into the Rhine. I never was in a greater crush. Thank God I, with Robertson, Moscheles and Dr Backer, an advocate at Vienna (deputy from there to this Festival) got safely on board, where we had 2 or 300 People all invited by the *Committee*, many of whom were on the Wharf (Blue ribbons on) to prevent any coming on board but those who had the Pass Tickets (which we had) from the Committee. Amidst the firing of cannon from our Vessel and the Shore, also from a Steam Vessel that came from Holland I suppose, full of passengers, the Ship was christened 'L. van Beethoven' by a Roman Catholic priest. I could scarcely see the ceremony for the crowd, but I smelt the Incense. A curious custom is for some Lady to be wedded to the Ship, a most elegantly dressed young Lady was the one selected for this occasion, who was just before me in the crowd when coming on board, she screamed very much; with great difficulty an Officer and a Soldier protected her. After the ceremony of Christening she left the Vessel escorted by a Gentleman full Dressed (a rare thing here) with the Priest finely Dressed, preceded by 2 boys carrying Candles and a Man dressed as our Parish Clerks are. On we went, firing away, crowds on the Shore and in the Hotels waving hats and Handkerchiefs.

Jules Janin, of the *Journal des Debats*, showed Davison his account of the day before sending it to Paris. The 'curious custom' alluded to by Smart is romantically expanded in Janin's opening paragraph:

On Monday the 11th, the crowd assembled on the borders of the Rhine to assist at the baptism of the 'Ludwig van Beethoven'. The new steam-boat merited the honor of such Baptism at the hands of such a people. The waters of the Rhine, swelled by the incessant rain – the high mountains capped with a feudal tower in the style of a ducal coronet – the two banks of the river crowded with people singing and clapping their hands – adorable majesty of great prospects and great deeds – immense river – immense people – immense exhibition of national pride – all these things made, indeed, a noble spectacle. On the fore deck of the vessel, all in white like a bride, modest and proud at once, stood the youthful sponsor, a soft and tranquil German beauty – with a sweet regard for and a bearing gentle and chaste! O ship! thou canst now quit the port in full steam! Thou canst brave the caprices and storms of the river full of tumults, poesies, thoughts, sometimes of regret, always of hope. The winds are for thee, the waves obey thee, the port opens before thy inviolable prow – possess thyself, conqueror, of this haughty stream – fling to the cities of the shore, fling to the smallest hamlets, fling to the poplars of these numberless isles, thy joyous and undulating vapour. Go! – thy reign commences – fill thyself with all the joys of the voyage – carry in one berth the idler and the thinker, the merchant and the poet, the artist and the soldier, the scholar and the diplomatist, the Catholic priest and the disciple of Luther. Go! – thy hour is come! – obey, without fear, the signal of the beautiful girl, thy sponsor, who with charming gestures, bestows upon thee the greatest name of the town where Julius Caesar once encamped. The name of the young godmother of the 'Beethoven' is Mdlle de Bethmann Holwig.[1]

After the ceremony of christening the boat, organised by the Director of the *Cölner Dampfschifffahrts-Gesellschaft*

We landed at the Island of Nonnenwerth, where we had a *very bad* cold repast on the Island at the Hotel, formerly a Nunnery.

1. Anna, a daughter of Professor von Bethmann-Hollweg, once a tutor of Prince Albert (of England).

Dr Backer *would* treat me to the Wine, he *ordered*, 2 or 3 Bottles of Champagne, to which he stuck closely, but gave several glasses away. During the repast a very fine Band of the 28th Regiment (I came in the Vessel) who played beautifully in an adjoining Room. Robertson was obliged to eat in another Room as places were reserved by the Committee only for Moscheles, Backer, Fétis & myself etc. I was so disgusted with the eating that I left the Table to walk in this beautiful Island. I persuaded Robertson to go with me, he fared no better than I did, but the wine was good, being selected by the Committee, so said the Card – which see. In walking round the Island I gave a woman, a violin player, a 3 Pfennige Piece and I played 'God save the Queen' to her on her not very bad Violin. We had Lieder Tafel singing on board both going & returning. We left Bonn about 1/4 to one (the time mentioned was ½ past 11) and left the Island to return soon after 5. We got back to Bonn quickly with the steam. Those I knew on board were Dr and Made Spohr, Moscheles, Mr and Mrs Fétis, Dr Backer, Messrs Holz & Fishchoff.[2] The 2 latter dined with Beethoven when I did in 1825. Moscheles said that Fischoff was a distinguished Artist in Vienna, he had bushy black Whiskers and wore spectacles; also Miss Sibyl Novello[3] & [lacuna] with her, and there were many others that I knew by sight in the steam Vessel.

Holz played the Violin or Tenor in Beethoven's Quartets when I was at Vienna; he is now a director of the Music in some place at Vienna. He has a M.S. work of Beethoven's called *The Dervishes* [No. 3 of *Die Ruinen von Athen*. Op. 113], and wishes to sell Beethoven's violin & viola which he gave to Mr Holz.

A most charming Trip, except that one of the sailors knocked

---

2. Carl Holz (1798-1858) was the second violinist of the Schuppanzigh Quartet, a devoted friend of Beethoven (who chose Holz as his biographer but afterwards repented of having done so), and a heavy drinker. J. Fischhof came into possession of various Beethoven Mss which he deposited in the Royal Library in Berlin.

On f. 70 of his Diary Smart noted of Holz: 'I saw him during my visit to Vienne in 1827 – I gave him my card – His Friend, Mr Pinnock, London'; and of Fischhof: 'I believe I saw him at Vienne in 1827'. Smart had a lapse of memory; he should have written, of course, 1825.

3. Mary Sabilla Novello (d. 1904) was the sixth daughter of Vincent Novello. As a singer she was overshadowed by her sister Clara, and also handicapped by indifferent health. She was, however, among the singers engaged for this Beethoven Festival (see p. 79).

Robertson's hat over into the Rhine. Thro' Moscheles I borrowed a Cap – or rather a Gent of the Committee did – from the Captain of the Vessel, which I went with Robertson to return at the Steam Packet office (after he had bought another Hat soon after we landed, which cost only 12 shillings (English) it was a silk Hat).

We landed rather before 6, too tired to go by Railroad to Brühl, to hear several Bands play there upon the expected arrival of our Queen at some uncertain hour this Evening.

On the Island we met Messrs Barnett, Davison, Flowers and his Anglo-Saxon friend, also young Kenney & Wild Jun. who tried hard to get into our Vessel, but the Committee would not allow them to do so until they procured Cards stating they belonged to the Press. The Press are not too modest, they did not *come with us* but in another Steam Boat, some said also provided by the Committee, this I doubt.

After returning the Cap lent to Robertson we walked outside the Walls of the Town; very fine ruins disfigured with Houses built on the Walls.

After so bad a Luncheon we ordered some Veal Cutlets with excellently dressed Potatoes & A PINT of Wine only between Mr Robertson and myself: Had a very agreeable conversation with Mr Barnett (editor) upon musical and other subjects during Supper, after which I went to bed early being tired.

During our passage up the Rhine Moscheles said his wife preferred staying at Antwerp to avoid the danger and bustle at Cologne and Bonn etc. He had to tell me some curious anecdotes about Madame Pleyel who has left her husband for 100 others etc. She is a fine P.F. player *patronized* by Liszt.

A Gent, a Mr Latham, a new arrival at our Hotel, knew me, said he had been trying to persuade Sir A. Barnard[4] to come here. Sir A. is going to Italy.

Rather extraordinary that Moscheles should not have known an Air to be Meyerbeer's played by the Band during our repast on the Island; he lost a Louis d'or to Dr Backer, he wagered it *was* Meyerbeer's. Near together at the table close to me were Spohr and

4. A Court functionary who in 1843 had selected W. H. Elgar (father of Edward Elgar) to tune Queen Adelaide's pianos.

his Wife, Mr and Mrs Fetis, Moscheles and also Dr Backer. My right-hand unknown neighbour did not like my helping myself to a Dish near me 'till the proper time for so doing.

Meanwhile the main interest of the day had been centred elsewhere. When the British Royal party left their ship they travelled first as far as Malines, where they were welcomed by the King and Queen of the Belgians. Thence they passed through Liège and Verviers to be met at the Prussian frontier by Lord Westmorland, now Ambassador in Berlin, the Chevalier Bunsen, the Prussian representative in London, and a delegation from the Prussian Court. At Aachen they were greeted by the King of Prussia.

At Cologne the city had to be crossed by carriage. The Queen noted that it was handsomely festooned, and the proverbial and characteristic scents (see p. 41) were somewhat disguised by the gallons of *Eau de Cologne* that had been sprinkled about the streets by order of the authorities. A quarter of an hour after leaving Cologne the Queen and the Prince reached Brühl, where they were to stay in the Augustusburg – the great Baroque palace re-shaped for the Elector of Cologne by Johann Conrad Schlaun in the 1720's and further improved by François Cuvillies. The Queen of Prussia, the Princess of Prussia, the Archduke Friedrich of Austria, the Duchess of Anhalt-Dessau, and the rest of the Prussian Court awaited their English guests.

After having been received, the party went up the great dome-crowned staircase inserted in the house by Balthasar Neumann. From one of the salons they looked out into the park where, under the light of many and many-coloured lanterns, a *Zapfenstreich*, or tattoo, was being given. The musicians – estimated at 200 trumpets and 400 drums – were directed by Meyerbeer, and their programme included Mendelssohn's 'Wedding March', selections from Meyerbeer's new opera, *Ein Feldlager in Schlesien* (1844), and 'God save the Queen'. Lord Aberdeen, Her Majesty's Foreign Secretary, agreed with Queen Victoria that the National Anthem had never been better played.

Monarchy then had a better time of it in Germany than in England. Queen Victoria had not yet begun her rehabilitation of the institution, which through the reigns of George IV and William IV had sunk low in general esteem. Prince Albert, through no fault of his, was still regarded with profound hostility by the English press (see p. 98). Both he and the Queen were for many reasons glad to be in Germany. Immediately, Albert greatly looked forward to showing his young wife many places that had been familiar to him not so many years before. Brühl was one of these places, and he related to her how he used to visit there when he was a student in Bonn between 1838 and 1840.

# CHAPTER 8

# The Unveiling of the Statue

Tuesday, August 12th

'Inauguration'.   About 6 o'Clock in the morning Mr Simrock, our
Landlord, came up to say that the Committee desired him to say to
the invited Guests in his Hotel, that we were to join the Procession
at the 'Belle Vue Hotel' at 8 this morning. A Gentleman at Breakfast
said he could not get back from Brühl until 2 o'Clock this morning
owing to the confusion with the Trains, he paid for a First Class place
and with difficulty got into the 3rd or 4th Class. He thinks there were
7000 persons at Brühl. Our Queen arrived there about 6 o'Clock
yesterday Evening, the Gent said. She did not show herself from the
Palace. He only heard a little of the music, he thinks more persons
went from Cologne to Brühl than from Bonn; hundreds were left to
get back to either place as they could. About 2 o'Clock there was a
violent knocking at our Hotel Gates. Simrock told me that about 12
persons would come in to sleep in the *Coffee Room* as they could not
have Beds. They came from Brühl and so hungry that they ate
upwards of 60 Pieces of Bread besides other things. It was most
fortunate that Robertson and I determined *not* to go to Brühl after
our return from the Steam Vessel expedition. The Gentleman thought
that one third of the Crowd at Brühl was English. At the Table
d'Hôte an English gentleman said there were 500 in all of the
Military Bands.

The procession to the cathedral, with the exception of the distinguished guests, assembled in the garden of the Zur schönen Aussicht (Belle Vue) Inn, with musicians, members of the shooting fraternity, and students (in groups of four), as described by Smart, at the head. Behind them were committee members. Then came the guests of honour who were picked up at the Town Hall. Behind them were the civil and military authorities of Bonn, representatives of the Churches, Professors and other members of the teaching profession, a student delegation, a delegation of the citizenry, a band, more citizens, and finally another body of military.

At 1/4 past 8 we went to the Town Hall, instead of the Hotel 'Belle Vue' with Moscheles, to wait for the Procession coming from Hotel 'Belle Vue' to pick us up, and to put the Gents assembled by invitation at this Town Hall in the center of the Procession. It was headed by a Military Band and corps of jaegers. Next came about 300 of the College Students and the captains of them in curious costumes, long Boots, with Spurs, Sword and Sashes, with Caps to correspond with the various colours and a kind of Fustian Jackets. No Flags in the Procession. When we came to the Minster door the Scholars made a lane for us Grandees to pass through. My *Coat* here and everywhere was treated with great respect. The moment the Procession got into the Minster the Scholars and crowd rushed in like thunder, nearly carrying the Dragoons' Horses in [with them] all. We were especially seated on a Sopha near the altar. Next to me was *Wolf* the Poet who wrote the Cantata Litzt [*sic*] set – (he is connected with our Athenaeum News Paper). Then Spohr. Next to me, on the left, was Robertson and close to him, standing, was Haehnel who carved Beethoven's statue. Fétis and Moscheles were near us. The crowd was great but we were luxuriously seated, Liszt in front of us standing. 4 priests, superbly drest did the duty, which began about 1/4 past 9 and was over at ½ past 10. The Mass went well, much better than at Rehearsal. Dr Breidenstein conducted but as he and the performers were behind the Altar we could not see them. The London Press pushed themselves in, I believe *without* invitation from the Committee. The Ladies were admitted by Ticket, before the great Door was opened and were seated in Pews. We *got out* at a side door in any way we could; I kept behind Spohr's great back. We were requested to meet again in the Town Hall to go again in procession to the 'Tribune' but as we had bought tickets for certain seats there, we determined to cut this 2nd Procession and go to our own seats. Well we did so for when the Procession entered they got seats (I suppose reserved for them) but not so good as ours.

The fact that the choir and orchestra were out of sight in the sanctuary (behind a temporary altar that had been erected for the day) prevented Smart (and others) from becoming aware of another crisis in Breidenstein's life. At the last moment he learned that Staudigl, the appointed bass soloist, would not be able to appear. By royal command Staudigl had been at Brühl the previous night, and in the morning had been held up through missing the train. Breidenstein, although advised that there were eminent singers who could stand in, wisely relied on an amateur in the neighbourhood who knew the part. So it was that a Herr Letellier joined Tuczek, Kratky and Herr Peretti, a local tenor.

Meanwhile the royal party at Brühl had breakfasted and driven to the railway station, thence by train to Bonn, and from the station there to von Fürstenberg's house. Here Professors Salomon (Vice-Chancellor of the University), Bethmann-Hollweg (whose pretty daughter was better known in the town than her father), and Walther, were presented to Queen Victoria. They had all been previously known to Prince Albert in his student days. Down below in the crowded Münsterplatz the band played overtures and excerpts from symphonies by Beethoven. But, as Breidenstein noted, only those nearest to the musicians heard anything.

A most beautiful morning during the Ceremony. Our Queen, with the King & Queen of Prussia with Prince Albert, arrived soon after 11, ½ an hour later than was appointed. They came in 4 or 5 Carriages from Brühl. There was a delay in the Royal Party coming into the balcony at Count Somebody's house, the People were impatient, but when they appeared (our Queen in a Pink Bonnet) the cheering was great. The Ceremony began with a Speech (from a Paper) by Dr Breidenstein without his hat. At the end of it the Statue was suddenly uncovered, the Sun broke forth at the moment.

The Shouts of the immense number of People, the Beating of Drums, the ringing of Bells and Cannons at a distance, the loud reports, all had a grand effect.

Then followed a dull piece of music, composed & conducted by Dr Breidenstein, accompanied by Wind Instruments only, and sung by Male Voices only, tho' all the Female Chorus singers were seated in front of the Statue (which is a good likeness of Beethoven) by Haehnel of Dresden Cast by Burschmidt [Burgschmiet] of Nuremburgh.

I am sure that the Royal Party were too far off to hear one word of Dr B's speech, or any of the Music, perhaps they might have heard the Drums when the music ended. The Royal Party retired into the House amidst the cheering of the Crowd, then many of the Committee and Spohr signed a Paper on the Monument, which Robertson thought would be enclosed in it, but I saw Dr B. reading it aloud, and so ended this interesting ceremony. The whole was excellently well managed. The Horse Soldiers rode round the 'Tribune' to keep back the crowd. Every seat in it was taken by Tickets to go to a seat on a Numbered Bench as written on the Card. All the Captains of the Colleges, or whatever they are called in their curious dresses, were together behind us. I did not see more than 2 or 3 of the College Boys with them. These Captains were very fine young men and they behaved extremely well.

Before the Ceremony a Pickpocket was apprehended for stealing a Ring he was taken near us. They said he was a Frenchman, he look'd very pale; the Gents of the Committee were looking at his Passport, the Police, dressed like Soldiers, took him away. There have been many Robberies besides young Wild's. They snatched a valuable pin from the shirt of Mr M. Barnett as he was coming out of the Church this morning – after the Grand Mass there.

For Queen Victoria the unveiling of the Beethoven statue was but one item on a long fixture-list. She wrote in her *Journal* how:

We stepped on to the balcony to see the unveiling of Beethoven's Statue, in honour of which great festivities took place, concerts &c. But, unfortunately, when the statue was uncovered, its back was turned to us. The *Freischützen* fired *a feu de joie,* and a chorale was sung. The people cheered us, and dear Albert most particularly, who is beloved here; and the band played a 'Dusch' at the same time, which is a flourish of trumpets, and is always given in Germany, when healths are drunk, &c. From here we drove with the King and Queen, – only a few of our suite following – to Albert's former little house. It was such a pleasure for me to be able to see this house. We went all over it, and it is just as it was, in no way altered. . . . We went into the little bower in the garden, from which you have a beautiful view of the Kreuzberg, a convent situated on the top of a hill. The *Sieben Gebirge* (Seven Mountains) you also see, but the view of them is a good deal built out.

Dr Breidenstein's twenty minute speech having been inaudible (as even its author conceded) it was duly printed in the commemorative volume concerning the occasion. After the unveiling of the monument Breidenstein conducted the first (and last) performance of his setting, for male voices and wind instruments, of an Ode written for the occasion by Wilhelm Smets of Aachen. The first fifty bars, said Davison, were listened to, the rest being treated with a deserved indifference. The words, however, were well attuned to the patriotic mood of the times –

> *Du Meister bist's, der Töne Hort!*
> *Das hohes Bild*
> *Vor unsern Augen ward enthüllt,*
> *An diesem Ort*
> *Wo deine Wiege stand,*
> *Denn hier bei uns am deutschen Rhein,*
> *Ob jedes Land dich nenne sein,*
> *Gewalt'ger, ist dein Vaterland.*[1]

Liszt's cantata should have been performed before this morning's ceremony. But when Breidenstein first saw the score he decided that an out-of-doors performance would have been too hazardous. Performance of this work, therefore, was postponed.

Before the crowds dispersed all the prominent persons present signed a parchment recording the occasion. Just before this was placed in the leaden casket prepared for it Professor Walther called out that there was

1. Thou art music's master and protector! The great image has been unveiled in our presence in the place where thou wert born. For here on the German Rhine, though every land calls you mighty, is your Fatherland.

present an Englishman, born in the same year as Beethoven, who had helped to establish the fame of Beethoven in England, and who should also add his name to the document. 'I ascended the steps of the pedestal,' wrote William Gardiner, 'and with a trembling hand would have written my name; but there was scarcely room. There was, however, a space just under Victoria and Albert, all and one cried out "Anglais! Anglais!" and I was ordered to write my name there – an honour I could never have expected, and the greatest I ever received in my life.' The casket containing this document was to be entombed within the monument. It was preceded to its last resting-place by the score of Dr Breidenstein's composition. This, however, did not need lead to weigh it down, its own weight being sufficient – as Davison rudely observed.

We had to wait a long time for our Table d'Hôte, until nearly 2 o'Clock. Both our Rooms crowded, perhaps 200 among the many who came hoping to find a place were Crevelli and Ferrari; they said they could not get a Dinner in Bonn. I did not stay to the end of the Dinner but brushed myself up to go to the Concert announced to begin at 6. It commenced at ½ past 6, over at a 1/4 to 9 – See Bill. Owing to the ticket Dr Breidenstein (had given me) for letter A we had capital places. Robertson got by, by saying he belonged to me, we were close to the Royal Box, among all the great Guns. Made. Spohr was just behind me next to Moscheles, old Ries came in with Mons. le Conseiller Wegeler, Beethoven's friend whom I dined with at F.Ries's at Godesberg in 1825. I was introduced to him at the Town Hall this morning by our Simrock's Brother (who apologised for not being at home – (fudge) – when I called upon him but the Conseiller remembered our meeting at Godesberg. I was delighted to talk with old Mr Ries after the Concert, he seemed to have enjoyed the music so much; everybody spoke to him. Mr Hallé, the Pianiste, who was in London, made himself known to me.

I forgot to observe that in the 'Tribune' this morning I was introduced to Herr Schindler, who wrote Beethoven's Life. I gave him my address in London. I believe he lives in Cologne. He was pleased to say that my name is well known in Germany. (I must say that my reception from all exceeds my expectations and is most flattering.) He laid it into Moscheles, who is, as he states, shown up in the 12th edition of his work, that is Beethoven's Life.

The afternoon concert began at 4 o'clock. The first part was conducted by Spohr at Liszt's request. Liszt found so much of his time occupied with committee meetings and other such tedious affairs that he was glad to be able to delegate some part of his artistic responsibility. In any case Spohr was universally popular.

The misfortunes of the organisers continued. Mantius, the tenor who should have sung the opening Christus recitative and aria from *The Mount of Olives* was not allowed to come. The King of Prussia required his services for a private concert at Brühl in honour of Queen Victoria (which was why Peretti had sung in the Mass), and in spite of Breidenstein making personal application to Meyerbeer, the Royal Music Director, for his release this could not be arranged. It was remarked that while the King showed a fine regard for his English guests he showed rather less for Beethoven.

The First Act of the concert (attended by *c* 2100 persons) consisted of the *Coriolanus* overture, the canon from *Fidelio*, the 'Emperor' Concerto, in which Liszt was the soloist, and the first section (with omissions for reasons stated below) of *The Mount of Olives*, in which Tuczek was said to have distinguished herself.

After the Fifth Symphony, the Second Act under Liszt's direction, continued with a String Quartet in E flat, (Op. 74?). This was played by Hartmann, Derkum, Weber, and Breuer, of Cologne. The performance, it was acknowledged, was of the highest order, with a perceptivity and sense of expression that was not so often otherwise shown during the Festival. By the time the Finale to *Fidelio* was reached many among the audience had had enough and departed.

> After Spohr had conducted the 1st Act he came and sat with us to be near his wife. By the bye there was rather too much Drumming and Trumpeting to Spohr & Liszt, who had some Bouquets thrown to them by the Chorus Girls (very good looking, all dressed in White) for the Festival was in honor of Beethoven *not* of Spohr and Liszt as my liberal Wine Friend from Vienna Dr Backer justly observed. *He* took much notice of Moscheles but few others did except Spohr. He

does not seem popular here. However he was very kind to me. I tried to get out between the Acts but could not the crowd being so great and it rained hard.

The concert went well but Spohr took the last movement of the chorus in 'The Mount of Olives' slow, perhaps he was afraid to push so large an orchestra. The Programme (which see) was much deranged. Spohr said the Quartet was played *before* the Sinfonia in the 2nd Act because they would be too much fatigued to play it as placed in the programme.

Why Liszt played the Concerto before the Canon I did not hear. Herr Beyer did not arrive from Brühl, therefore the Introduction and Tenor Aria in 'The Mount of Olives' were omitted and no apology was made; they would not have allowed this in London without some explanation. I doubt if half the room could have heard the Quartet which was beautifully played, Spohr said the 4 Players were from Cologne. It was curious to see Liszt get up after the first part of the Concerto and walk about the orchestra, bowing to the applause. Spohr shook hands with him, then he sat down and finished the concerto.

The Rev Mr Shannon, formerly at Edinburgh, spoke to me, he did not like the 2nd so well as the 1st Concert nor did I. Made Dulcken[2] gave a broad hint to sit in my place. I advised her, certainly in no polite manner, to find a seat further on; Mr Dulcken said he was glad to see me in his country! I spoke to Mr Hodgson, Messrs Davison and Kenney and Flower & Gruneison got into our A seats. I overheard Davison tell Mr Feemy or Famy (who sleeps in the same room with Barnett in our Hotel) he is the Morning Herald Reporter, that they got into this best place by saying, 'The Queen sent them.' Too bad this, but the Press Gang here do not stick at trifles.

I forgot to observe in my description of the Great Hall that in the center of ⭕ all round the Room there is one of Beethoven's

---

2. Louisa Dulcken (1811-50), sister of Ferdinand David, was a pianist and a well-known teacher. After her marriage in 1828 she lived in London.

works mentioned. In the one over the orchestra the date of his Birth in Bonn and of his death in Vienna, and a good portrait of him.

It fortunately did *not* rain in coming home. We narrowly escaped being hurt, as many must have been by the rascally conduct of a Gentleman's Coachman who *would* drive furiously up to the door amidst the crowd of Ladies & Gents coming out. What would Margaret have done had she been with us! The 2 stupid Police Soldiers, instead of knocking him off the Box, which would have been done and properly so in London, kept pulling the Horses back by the Reins, while the Coachman was whipping them on, this of course frightened the poor Animals. It was a mercy that hundreds were not killed. How it ended I know not for we got out of the crowd and took Coffee, and then intended to walk out to see the whole Town illuminated. I am now writing with 6 Candles in my Window – a Band playing in the Market Place – bad Fireworks are being let off, but it is a gay scene from here. So ends this busy day – and thank God that Robertson and I have escaped from the many accidents there must have been.

Sir George's expenditure had diminished, although the interest of his accounts increased.

f. 79v.

| | |
|---|---|
| August 10 – Rehearsal in Hall | 15 |
| Programme of 1st Concert | $2\frac{1}{2}$ |
| Letter to Margaret | $6\frac{1}{2}$ |
| Goute [*sic*] at the Island of Nonneneworth | 20 |
| August 12 The Washerwoman brought to me in my Room as I was going to Bed the 4 Neckhank: I sent to be washed. She charged 4 Groschen but as I had no changed [*sic*] I gave her | 5 |

After leaving the morning ceremonies the royal party had inspected Prince Albert's former rooms and the various exhibitions. In the afternoon there was a banquet at Brühl at which the King paid graceful tribute to Queen Victoria. After that there was a firework display in Cologne, which the royal guests watched from a steamer on the river. The evening was in no way spoiled, it was said, by a continuous drizzle. It was after midnight when the party returned to Brühl.

# CHAPTER 9

# 'Hamlet' mostly without the Prince of Denmark

August 13, Wednesday

I put out my 6 Candels last night soon after 10, as all my
Neighbours opposite seemed to do so. The Music & Fireworks
ceased about that time. It was a gay scene with the Flags and Green
wreaths with Candles in all the Houses. I found Simrock lighting
candels in a Room near mine (which were ready lighted when I came
in after the Concert.) Simrock said he had so much to do that he was
no longer Master of his own house. He and his Wife seem to be
worthy people. She is rather plain but polite, and speaks a little
French also English I believe. Robertson laughed at my
misunderstandings the Keller [*sic*], who replied to my question
'Where is Herr Simrock?' 'Er schläft' (He sleeps) – which I mistook
and said to Robertson, 'What does he shave for at this time of day
just after dinner?' I laughed when informed he was *sleeping*.

   I must not forget that I gave my London address to Dr Backer
(Moscheles' friend) of Vienna, & Mr Fétis of Brussels, and to Mr
Schindler. We met Miss Sybil Novello and Mrs Guscel on our
return from the Tribune yesterday, they had not been there or at the
Church.

On Wednesday morning the guests at Brühl should have been in Bonn
by 9 o'clock, for that was when the 'Artists' Concert' was timed to
begin. An early start was deemed necessary because of the time required
to be otherwise set aside during the day for eating and drinking. Instead

of being in Bonn, however, the house-party was still at breakfast in Brühl. It arrived at the concert more than an hour and a half late. The first movement of the Festival Cantata specially composed for the Festival had already been sung when the royal guests arrived and made their appearance. In addition to those already mentioned there were present the Duke of Anhalt-Cöthen, the Counts of Stollberg and Redern, the Earl of Westmorland and Alexander von Humboldt. The Cantata, which lasted 45 minutes, was begun afresh after the interruption and the performance of the Prussian national anthem *Heil Dir im Siegerkranz*.

The Cantata, for those who noticed the details (and Smart was not among them), was to a specially prepared text by Wolf which predictably ended thus:

*Heil! Heil! Beethoven Heil!*

It was scored for 4 soloists (Sachs, Schloss, Götz, Staudigl), chorus, and large orchestra, the latter including valve-horns (exceptional at that date) and harp. There being no harpist the part was transferred to piano and played by Kapellmeister Dorn (once Schumann's teacher in Leipzig) of Cologne. The work impressed the professionals by the quality and originality of the instrumentation, and the general public (attendance *c* 2350) by the clever way in which Liszt had taken part of the slow movement[1] of the 'Archduke' Trio (Op.97) and dressed it up for voices and instruments for exhibition in a new setting.

The disruption of the time-table continued. Indeed any attempt to provide what had been advertised in the stated order was at once renounced. After Liszt's Cantata 'it was left to the two Queens to make the selection of the next musical pieces which were to be performed in their presence. It was thus, that not only the pieces of the programme were changed from their announced order of succession, but several of the pieces were necessarily wholly omitted on account of the delay that had thus occurred; and the musical part of the festival was brought to a termination in a somewhat unsatisfactory manner, and without a real and proper conclusion in the opinion of a majority of the audience. A few, however, among whom was *Spohr*, received an invitation to the

1. Breidenstein wrote that it was the *second* movement (*Zur Jahresfeier...*, 1846, p.21).

grand concert, to be given by the King of Prussia in honour of his exalted guests at Brühl that night'.[2]

When the Queens had consulted together after the end of Liszt's Cantata and Prussia had tactfully invited Victoria to determine the items to follow, the latter with equal tact requested music by Beethoven. It was, of course, not easy to comply with that request. However the overture to *Egmont* was played and, separated from it by a doleful cello solo by Ganz and Weber's *Concertstück* played with verve by Berlioz's one-time *inamorata* Marie Pleyel, 'Abscheulicher', from *Fidelio*, was sung by Sabilla Novello. This was the point at which protocol allowed an exodus of the royal party, already late for their next appointment in the University Aula. Queen Victoria had heard music by Beethoven; while the Prussian King and Queen had listened to the English singer, whose little voice was hardly to the taste of a German audience.

> *Account of 3rd Concert.* We got in good time to excellent places in
> Letter A. I sat next to two very pleasant German Ladies – I made
> them laugh at many of my remarks, particularly about the curious
> Dress of some Princess which looked like a Piece of Handkerchief:
> I called her the Princess de *Mouchoir.* They waited till 5 m past 10 for
> the Royal Party and then began (see Programme). Before they did so
> Professor Wolf, who wrote Liszt's cantata, made a speech requesting
> the Company not to get on the Benches for fear they should break
> down and cause accidents, however we saw many broken Benches as
> we went out. We were amused by fine Chairs etc being brought into
> the Royal Box almost at the last moment. A Prussian officer – at my
> (justly) admiring these Chairs (he was one of the Committee) seemed
> pleased.
>
> The Royal Party walked from the very bottom of the Room to
> the Royal Box at the top, a bad arrangement. The King of Prussia
> had our Queen on his arm, Prince Albert the Queen of Prussia, then
> followed Prince William of Prussia, with a host of Lords and Ladies,
> among them Lord Westmoreland (I did not see his Lady in this
> suite). He nodded to me from the Royal Box; in returning his nods
> I was afraid our Queen might think I intended them for her as he sat

2. *Louis Spohr's Autobiography*, p.272.

just behind her. I saw him pointing me out to Lord Liverpool.[3] In going out Lord Westmoreland kindly shook hands with me, he had a Lady on his arm. During the performance the Queen, whose eyes were everywhere, pointed me out to Prince Albert. Gruneison and Robertson said 'Look, Prince Albert is telling the King of Prussia who you are.' I think it was so, for all the Royal eyes were upon me, the King with his glass; he went to the Chorus Girls in the most familiar manner, I suppose he desired them to send someone to him that he might order what was to be performed; such a derangement of the Programme could not have been done in England.

It seems that Moscheles was asked, but declined, to accompany 'Adelaide'; well he did for it was sung badly. Sib: Novello's voice sounded well, but she wanted esprit for so great a song. Ganz[4] – Cello, is not so great as Lindley,[5] Möser,[6] violin, pupil of De Bériot, has talent; he played the Paganini Pizzicato tricks, both these Gents introduced airs of Mozart, etc. with Variations. Franco-Maules the other Cello, a Jew told me at the table d'hôte that it was the Band who hissed him and tore his Parts, because they were jealous of him; this may be, but he is inferior to the other Cello who played, Ganz – Made Pleyel played Weber's Concertstück better than I have yet heard it, with much taste and plenty of force. Mlle Schloss sung well.

When the Royal Party went, the Orchestra and Company doubted if they were to go or stay; then there was a call for Staudigl. Some Gent got into the Conductor's place and said he was gone by command to Brühl. This was in bad taste and would have created a great row in England, besides he could have got to the King's Concert at Brühl in plenty of time after the Concert here – therefore I supposed he might be offended because the King did not

3. Charles Cecil Cope Jenkinson (1784-1851), third Earl of Liverpool, held the office of Lord Steward from 1841-6.
4. Moritz Ganz (1806-68), of Mainz, played in the Royal Orchestra in Berlin. In 1837 he played at a Philharmonic Concert in London.
5. Robert Lindley (1776-1851), belonged to a musical family from Yorkshire, was principal cello at the Royal Opera and the greatest English virtuoso on that instrument at that time.
6. August Möser was the son of Carl Möser (1774-1851), Royal Kapellmeister in Berlin.

ask for his song this morning. However, after the Speech away went
the Company, who with the Performers seemed tired with the
quantity of Music during the week. This was not a good Concert
but the Royalty being present satisfied all but us Professors; there
were plenty of us in letter A place either invited or thrust themselves
in. Mrs Oury stuck herself into a front row. I had every reason to be
satisfied with the attention I received from all the Professors and from
the officials, and I was highly satisfied with my place next to the two
German laughing Ladies. Spohr was down in the Room and then up
in the Orchestra when required, his slow movements from the Room
to the Orchestra, caused a delay not desirable either to the Royal
Persons or to the Public.

Queen Victoria left a brief account of the concert. 'Unfortunately', she
wrote,

though very well executed, there was but very little of Beethoven; – only
part of one of the Symphonies, brought into a Cantata by Liszt, and the
Overture to Egmont directed by Spohr. From here we drove to the University, where were drawn up all the Professors, who were all presented to me,
and many of who had taught my beloved Albert, and spoke with pleasure and
pride of my all in all – Professor Harrles, Professor Perthes (from Gotha),
Professor Arndt, a most distinguished and amiable old man – Professor
Breitenstein [sic]...Several of the students were there in the fine dress they
wore at the Beethoven Festival, with the rapier in their hands; many fine young
men, with loose hair, and beards and moustaches, and most with Säbelhiebe
[sword-cuts] across their faces. It interested me exceedingly.

After the concert had ended those who had been invited to the final
banquet hurried to the Goldener Stern, where a spate of speeches gave
cause for fresh animosities, as Smart reported.

We got out and to the Hotel much better than last night, being
daylight, no Rain. Had but just time to get to the Great union of the
Artists etc. at the Table d'Hote at the 'Grand Hotel d'Etoile d'or.'
Dinner began about ½ past 2 – about 500 Persons dined, the dinner
nothing extraordinary (not so good as at our hotel) but it must have
been difficult to provide for so many. A great Crowd & pushing to

get into the Room at a small door, where all those who had not promised to dine there were prevented entered [*sic*]. Liszt had put down our names at his table (See the Card) and we found our names in plates. Near us were Herr Wolf, the Poet; Bishopp [he means Fischoff] of Vienna, where I had met him; Blasis, the Clarinet player and his wife, Made Meerti, Gruneison & Franco-Maules, the Cello, who remembered me when in London with Hummel. Behind us was Herr Holz of Vienna with his English friend, Mr Pinnock, and a chubby musical Professor whose name I did not hear. There was an excellent Band in the gallery.

5 long Tables in the Room we dined in – another room joined on at the bottom of ours, very fine large Room with 2 Galleries in it, one opposite the other. It was well ventilated at top. A fountain began to play all over the company seated at one Table. It was soon stopped. The Tables were placed and presided at thus [*see opposite*]

Not very long after we began eating, Toasts were given by Wolf, Spohr, Liszt, Dr Breidenstein and others. It seems that Liszt in his 1st speech complimented *all* nations except the French, in his 2nd speech, having been privately told of his omission, he praised the French from whom he had received such kindness. However, this omission caused dissatisfaction among the French, who, with the Jews, are not popular here. (Franco-Maules, the Cello, is a Jew) Then began a row caused by Wolf the poet (who they said was also a Jew) who would speak (after having given 2 or 3 toasts) and they would not hear him but called for Spohr who got up and sat down again he being not inclined to speak.

The uproar during the speeches was considerable, so that it was not to be wondered at that Smart left. When Breidenstein spoke he was interrupted by those who wished to show their disapproval of his efforts and that of the Committee. Wolff was thoroughly excited and his discomfiture amid the fumes of champagne and cigar smoke was entirely distasteful. The cause of peace was not helped when it was forgotten to toast the Queen of England. French Flowers, 'burning with loyalty and patriotism', immediately drew Spohr's attention to the omission, which was at once repaired.

## Speeches.

Room with 2 Galleries in it one
opposite the other — it was well
ventilated at top, a fountain
began to play, all over the company
seated at one Table it was soon stopped,
the Tables were placed and presided at
thus

not very long after we began eating
Toasts were given by Wolf, Spohr,
Liszt Dr Breidenstein and others, it seems
that Liszt in his 1st Speech complimented
all nations except the French, in
his 2d Speech having been privately told
of his omission he praised the French

At the side tables the Frenchmen present were murmuring insolences concerning the Germans. For obvious reasons there was no love lost between the two nations. Davison was much entertained by a story passed on to him by Jules de Glimes. Breidenstein, the story went, told a friend that he had written a work in honour of Beethoven, and asked whether the friend would go to hear it. 'I shall not be able to do so', replied the friend, 'but if you were dead and Beethoven had composed a work in your honour I should make a point of going to hear it.'

This row was noisy, and fearing we might get into a scrape we left the Room. When complaining in the yard that we did not know whom we were to pay for our Dinner a Masonic Englishman, who knew me, tho' I did not know him, said he would settle this for me and lend me money if I required it. I declined his kind offer and we determined to call and pay to-morrow. We took leave of Mr and Mrs Spohr in going out of the Room, they expect to go to Cassel to-morrow, he said he might be in England next Summer. Surely the King of Prussia ought to command him to come to the Concerts at Brühl with the other great Artists.

We saw Messrs Ferrari, Crevelli & Magrath in the room and Messrs Flowers and Kenney junior. I concluded *all* our English Friends were there though we did not see them. What would our English Ladies say to dining with such a number of Good and bad Characters each talking to the other without ceremony or introduction. In going into the Room we were glad to take Miss S. Novello and Made Guscel and put them into their seats at the Table. There we left them to find our places. It was a curious, noisy Dinner.

I was glad to hear from Herr Schindler, who wrote Beethoven's Life (which Moscheles *said* he translated),[7] that Mr Ries had that day been made a Doctor in consequence of his own worth, and having been the intimate friend of Beethoven and the father of the talented F. Ries. This will be gratifying news to Jos. Ries. We were detained longer at the Hotel where we dined in consequence of the Rain. I saw Schlesinger of Paris, who had dined there. I spoke to him before

7. Schindler makes it quite clear that in his view Moscheles claimed much more than he was entitled to in respect of his association with Beethoven. See A. F. Schindler, *Beethoven as I knew him*, ed. D. W. MacArdle, trans. C. S. Jolly, London 1966, pp. 371-4.

at one of the Concerts. He wanted me to go with him to Coblentz to the Fetes to be given there in consequence of our Queen being at the King of Prussia's Castle at Stolzenfels.

We saw Moscheles going up to his Room from the Dinner Table, he said, 'I am ashamed of my Countrymen!' I conclude he did not like the remarks about the Jews which he must have heard. It seems that the Germans are very angry with us for *emancipating* the Jews as they term it.[8]

I forgot to observe that in going into the dining Room with Made Guscel on my arm I kept the Princess de *Mouchoir's* Dress out of the wet on the pavement, proper politeness on my part, for which this ugly Princess returned me thanks in French.

Robertson and I went to the Casino, we were admitted there by the card which Dr Breidenstein gave us. In the 1st room to which we went they were playing at Billiards, there were two tables. A Bishop from Vienna, who walked with us in the procession from the Town Hall, was looking at the Players. Out of this room was a Room where they were eating and Drinking. Simrock said that things might be had there à la carte, of course by the members only of the Club. I presume like our Club Houses. We then went into two Reading Rooms and from thence into a queer Garden with a bit of a Fountain in it. Some Gents were in a Room with a long passage in it fitted up for some sort of Game with Balls. Robertson said that they gave entertainments to the Ladies occasionally at these Cassinos [*sic*]. The House seem'd large but it cannot be compared with the elegance of our Club Houses.

We returned to our Hotel to take Coffee before going to the Ball in the Great Music Hall. While we [were] at Coffee Mr Gruneison told us of a quarrel *he* got into at the Dinner *we* left in consequence of the row. A Gent told him he might 'go to Hell' – upon which Gruneison demanded his card. The Gent refused to give it, upon which Gn. drew his Glove across the Gent's face which the said Gent

8. Some disabilities had been removed from the Jews in Britain after 1830. Jews had been admitted to certain professions and offices, and in 1837 the philanthropist Moses Montefiore (1784-1885), a Sheriff of the City of London, was knighted. In 1844 Nathan Adler (1803-90), a German scholar and theologian, became the first Chief Rabbi of British Jews.

did not resent and so the affair ended. Query? What sort of a Gent was he, supposing G's account to be correct? He said that he had had another disagreeable affair since that of the Glove, but it was settled. I am not surprised at his getting into scrapes for he cannot keep quiet for 5 minutes, besides this his manners are very abrupt.

It rained hard, therefore we gave up going to the Ball, but while we were doubting as to our going or not Robertson's Nephew arrived from London. He got to our Hotel while we were at the Cassino (about 6 o'Clock). He had a rough passage from Dover to Ostend in a *small* Vessel with 60 Passengers. He could not come in the 'Odine' as the Boiler burst. He slept at Liege. The Trains were crowded, therefore their arrivals were much delayed. He saw our Queen etc. at Cologne today at 4. She must have gone there *after* the Concert here. He says the Streets were crowded, and 300 young Girls were dressed in White, strewing flowers as the Royal Carriages passed. He agrees with us that the Queen does not look well. But the ladies are all charmed with Prince Albert. *He* looked well in our Field Marshal's uniform; the blue regimental dress of the Prussian Officers is not fine.

As the rain prevented our going to the Ball we went to our Rooms early. And so ends the Festival doings – and very bad was the ending as to the Concert today and the row at the Table d'Hôte at the Golden Star.

Within the area of conflict which was one of the distinguishing features of this Festival the personality of Liszt provided constant substance for acrimony. Liszt's bitterest critics, so Davison said, were the French journalists who had not only lived out of Liszt's pocket, but had also borrowed money from him for their return fares. His bill at the Goldener Stern was reported to have amounted to some 11,000 francs. Having previously provided 14,000 francs towards the cost of the monument, of the Beethoven Hall (which was his idea), and the ceremonies, he was perhaps justified in feeling somewhat indignant at the way matters in general were conducted.

That night there was a Ball in the Beethoven Hall in Bonn, at which 1100 people were present. When the function ended it was 1 o'clock on

Thursday morning. It was raining hard, and there were no carriages to be had, so the guests departed with dampened spirits.

During the afternoon Queen Victoria and Prince Albert again visited Cologne, where they were received before the cathedral by Archbishop Geissel in full canonicals, and there the plans for and progress towards the completion of the great building were explained to them. Then they went back to Brühl for the last time, delighted that their relatives, the King and Queen of the Belgians, were to join them for the concert which Meyerbeer had organised for them. He had also composed a work in honour of the occasion. Apart from some piano pieces by Liszt, the programme comprised vocal music sung by Mantius, Pischeck, Staudigl, Lind, Viardot-Garcia, and Tuczek.[9]

9. Spohr, op. cit., p. 272.

# CHAPTER 10

# Sir George begins to pack

The Festival being over the Committee reviewed its achievements. Taking everything into consideration, it was thought with some complacency, the event had passed off pretty well, and there were some pleasing memories. Of these the one that gave the most satisfaction was the gesture of the Philosophical Faculty of the University in presenting old Ries with an honorary doctorate. He had done much for the city, and his sons Ferdinand and Hubert (orchestral leader in Berlin) had brought honour to it through their achievements. Right to the end Franz had taken part in musical activities with all the zest of a young man. He had been present at the start of the second of the Festival concerts, and it was a moving spectacle as he was led to his seat of honour by the only surviving companion of his youth, Dr Wegeler, and Herr Gerhard, a member of the Committee. The trumpeters of the orchestra sounded a fanfare.

When the accounts of the Festival were scrutinised it was seen that while the income was 12,900 Thaler, the expenses amounted to 15,793 Thaler – a deficit, therefore, of 2893 Thaler. The deficit was defrayed by members of the Committee and by the King of Prussia, who contributed 800 Thaler.

There was one remaining public duty. On Thursday morning a party assembled to witness the inauguration of two new streets in Bonn. Liszt had been invited to lay the foundation stone – which he did in the presence of a handful of journalists and citizens – including Schmidt, the proprietor of the *Stern*, the oldest inhabitant of the city, and the ubiquitous Wolff. As usual Wolff read a speech. After the naming of the streets – the one *Beethovenstrasse*, the other *Lisztstrasse* – the consumption of vintage Hochheimer from a common goblet, and a ceremonial shaking of hands all round, the company dispersed. Smart missed out on this function.

Thursday, August 14th

I had little sleep last Night owing to the noise of the Carriages coming from the Ball. About 5 this Morning I heard an hollowing [*sic*] in the Street. I got up to see the occasion of it, about 12 men were marching down the St from the Minster opposite our Hotel, shouting and singing. When they were in the Market Place they saw me looking at them in my Night Cap, they wished me 'good morning'. I thought it better to pop into bed, but by peeping, I saw them form a Ring around one of their Party, who seemed [to be] addressing them. They were then very quiet, and soon went away. The Flags are being taken down from the Houses. The modern improvements will soon destroy the old picturesque appearance of many of the tops of the Houses in this Town. [*see p. 90*]

Very wet morning; the poor Women in the Market place, with their long *White* Handkerchiefs covering their heads and coming a long way down their backs, protecting their necks from the Sun & wet, make a curious effect from the number of them. The Market before our house is well supplied with vegetables. The Potatoes and Salads are very fine, but they say the Potatoe crop has failed in Belgium by a sort of Blight. I hope it has not in England.

Went with Mr Robertson to put a letter in the Post for his Niece. On our return found a letter from Margaret which I anxiously expected. We then went to buy a Pr. of Gloves (very dear), as I had lost one Glove. I also bought a Picture of Godesberg and the island of Nonnenworth. We paid the Bill for our bad dinner yesterday at the Golden Star – a dear dinner. In coming home we saw the King of Prussia and a Gent in one carriage, and in another, our Queen & the Queen of Prussia with Prince Albert and someone else, going to embark in a Steam Vessel for the King of Prussia's castle, Stolzenfels, near Coblentz, very few Guards or Outriders. The Populace took

in the Market Place they saw me
looking at them in my Night Cap,
they wished me "good Morning." I thought
it better to pop into bed, but by peeping,
I saw them from a Being crossing one
of their Party, who seemed addressing them
they were then very quiet, and soon
went away — The Steps are being
taken down from the Houses the modern
improvements will soon destroy the
old picturesque appearance of many of the tops
of the Houses in this Town —

little notice of them. Young Robertson said there was not much of a crowd to see them embark; perhaps their coming was not known.

We walked to the place of embarkation to Coblentz, there we saw Miss S. Novello and her friend Made. Guscel (a good P.F. player. Robertson says, can play any of Beethoven's Sonatas by heart), preparing to start by the boat for Coblentz, where Miss S. N. is to sing and also at a concert at Emms [sic], to oblige someone in distressed circumstances. The King of Prussia's Chamberlain wrote a civil letter (to I suppose an application) full of regrets that he could not request her to sing at Stolzenfels as 3 Ladies from a distance had already been engaged. Miss Novello & her friend were much annoyed at 13 Napoleons having been stolen out of their Trunk at their *Private* Lodgings, supposed by the Maid Servant, whose lover was a *Locksmith*, therefore Love does not laugh *at* but *with* Locksmiths. This Servant was detected in wearing one of Miss Novellos White Dresses. Plenty of Robberies in Bonn during this Festival.

We saw Lord Westmoreland's Carriage on the Key waiting to be embarked for Coblentz – there were 2 Maid Servants and the same Foreign man Servant I saw when we crossed from Dover. I desired then to give my Comp$^s$. to Lord Westmoreland who with his lady, had followed the Royal Party to Stolzenfels, where 100$^s$ from Bonn seemed to be going, amongst whom was Crivelli, Ferrari and Mr and Mrs Fétis, whom I took leave of on the Key. He gave me his Card and said he had left one at the Hotel, which I found on my return there.

Mr Robertson got a £20 Bill exchanged at Mr Jonas Cahn's, the Banker. After an excellent and quiet dinner at our Table d'Hote I put a letter into the Post for Jos. Ries. We were stopp'd by the Rain, therefore stood for some time under the Booths erecting for the Fair to-morrow (close to Beethoven's Statue) where I bought *3 Gold Crosses* for the Ladies chez moi. We then went to the Rhine with the intention of crossing by the Flying Bridge but the continued Rain prevented this and the intended walk on the other side of the Rhine.

During our visit to Mr Ries this Morning, who gave me 2 Kisses On Parting, he told me an extraordinary anecdote of the King of Prussia having given a large sum to, and settled a Pension of about

£60 English, on Mr Schindler for some Ms. Music of Beethoven sold
to the King by Mr S. – but Mr Holz told Mr Ries, and showed him a
paper signed by a dozen Persons stating that Mr S. had taken this
Music and a Trunk containing other things from Beethoven's house
immediately after his death without permission from his Nephew or
anyone else. Mr Ries says this affair will be made public; if so, and the
assertion against Mr Schindler should be proved, Mr Moscheles will
be sufficiently revenged for all that Mr Schindler has said against him
for pirating his book of Beethoven's Life.

The rain continuing we could not go out, therefore we settled the
Account with Herr Simrock who had left out the charge for 2 or 3
Articles we had. The bill was moderate considering the Festival, but
quite enough, it was *lower* than the Agreement made with Mr Jos.
Ries. We were extremely comfortable before the arrival and after the
departure of the influx. My Bed Room was well enough, the bed
with French Curtains suspended from the top, a stove in the Room
for Winter, the Pipe for the Smoke conveyed thro' the Wall into the
Passage. I did not see a Fireplace like ours in any Room in the Hotel.
There was a Sopha, Chest of Drawers, a large Table without a Drawer
and a Washing Stand, the drawer stuck so it was no use. The Beds
are not made or the Slops emptied 'till late in the day, which is very
inconvenient. A Bell Rope in the Room, the Bell is soon answered for
it is usual in large Hotels to have a Waiter in attendance on every
Floor. Women are not often in attendance, tho I had a German,
French & English Conversation with a Droll Maid Servant about the
Night Light, which was a wick in a peice [*sic*] of tin floating in Oil;
sometimes a plain or an ornamented China outside – very good light –
Two Ladies were in the next Room to mine which I should think
they never left as I always saw them in it as I passed.

The Boots & Shoes are put outside the Bed Room door, which
you find there very early in the Morning well cleaned. You must
keep your room door lock'd and deposit the Key on a similar number
to your Room on a Board in the Eating Room. Visitors Cards are
stuck in your Key hanging up in this Board. They have not a good
plan about *receiving* letters, they are not put into a particular place
which they ought to be, but you must ask for them. The House for

an Hotel was clean but occasionally horrid smells in sundry and divers parts of it at the back where the Ducks etc. were enjoying themselves. Simrock makes up 80 beds he said. Began my packing before going to bed.

Sir George brought his finances up to date:

f. 79

| | T | G |
|---|---|---|
| Thursday, August 14 | | |
| Paid Mr Robertson for Band of Musicians in Hotel | | 2½ |
| Programme of Concerts | | 10 |
| Pair of Gloves | | 18 |
| Dinner yesterday at the Golden Star | 2 | 0 |
| View of Nonnenworth & Godesberg Castle | 1 | 15 |
| Settled the above with Mr Robertson in his Room August 14 | | |
| August 14 Postage of letter to Mr Jos:Ries | | 6½ |
| 3 Golden Crosses at the Stalls erecting in the Minster Place | | |
| for the Fair where each of many Articles was to be had | | |
| for 2½ Groschen | | 7½ |

f. 78v

On Thursday Night August 14, 1845, I settled with
Mr Robertson for my share of Herr Simrock's Account from
Thursday Morng; August 7th when we arrived at the Hotel de
Trêves to our departure on Friday Mn: August 15
*including* our Breakfasts on that Morning          T G P
My *Total* share was                                          46 14 6
which I paid Mr Robertson for in English Money £6 16 8½
deducting £— 19 7 for what Mr Simrock paid for me for
Postage, Book of Beethoven's Life – and for Tickets for *all*
the Performances – (these Tickets came to £– 15 –) my
Share for Board and Lodging for these 8 days was £– 14 7
3/4 per day.
N.B. – We dined out of Simrock's Hotel *3 times*.

It rained again during the morning but by the time the royal family had come from Brühl to Bonn and embarked on their steamer the skies had cleared. The vessel carried a rich cargo – of three Queens, two Kings, one Prince Consort, one Archduke, and the Crown Prince who was to become the first German Emperor with his Princess. Other notabilities aboard included Alexander von Humboldt. Past Coblenz at the fortress of Ehrenbreitenstein the royal party was greeted by salvoes of gun-fire, which came from 20,000 troops scattered about the hills and valleys. It was as impressive as it was frightening, and it started to rain again.

# CHAPTER II

# Homecoming

The mock medieval castle of Stolzenfels, a memorial to the bourgeois taste of the nineteenth century Prussian monarchy, was a gloomy place in which to be incarcerated. True, there were enchanting views in every direction, with abundant ruins crowning the hills above the river; but for a twenty-five year old girl the disciplines imposed by a State Visit were severe. Sometimes, one feels, too severe. There was a charming anecdote bruited among the journalists attached to that royal tour which bears on this.

The Queen had fallen out with the Prince and for half-an-hour they were not on speaking terms. At the end of this half-hour (it was said) the Queen knocked on the Prince's door. 'Who', he asked, 'is there?' 'The Queen.' The Prince did not speak. Five minutes later the same scene was re-enacted. Another five minutes elapsed and then the Queen knocked more timorously. 'Who's there?' asked the Prince once again. 'It's Victoria, Albert,' was the tearful response. The door was now opened, and the Queen rushed into the room and Albert's arms.

From Stolzenfels Victoria and Albert travelled back to the little dukedom whence the Prince derived his title and where he had been brought up. They travelled by way of Mainz, Aschaffenburg, Würzburg, Erfurt, Rossbrunn, Bamberg, and Coburg to Rosenau, which was the Prince's birthplace. It was altogether a sentimental journey and the Queen was greatly moved at every turn. Most of all, perhaps, when she saw the little room which Albert had shared with his brother Ernest under the stern eye of their tutor. It had been a Spartan upbringing.

They went into Coburg several times. One evening the local company performed Meyerbeer's *Les Huguenots*, at the end of which 'God Save the Queen' was sung to a German translation. On St Gregory's Day, celebrated in Coburg by a children's festival, there was a parade of 1300 pupils from the schools of the duchy before the Castle. The Queen was enchanted, writing in her *Journal*:

All the children marched two and two into the courtyard, headed by their schoolmaster and a band, the boys first, and then the girls, – some in costume as shepherdesses, &c., and a little boy in court dress and powder – and the greater part of the girls in white with green. Three girls came upstairs and presented us with a very pretty poem to the tune of 'God save the Queen,' – and which they sang extremely well... The children then marched off as they came. After this we drove to the Anger, a meadow close to the town. Here were pitched two tents, decorated with flowers, and open at the sides, under which we were to dine. All the children were in front of us. We walked round among them, and then sat down to dinner. A band of music played the whole time... The children danced – and so nicely and so merrily – waltzes, polkas, &c.; and they played games, and were so truly happy, – the evening was so beautiful, – the whole scene so animated, – the good people so quiet, it was the prettiest thing I ever saw.... We were all much struck by the number of pretty children. At six we drove back to the Palace.

On Sunday, 24 August, Victoria and Albert, with their Coburg relatives, drove into the town to hear *Hauptgottesdienst* in the Moritz-kirche. The pastor greeted the Queen who, he reminded her, was descended from the Saxon Dukes 'who were the first Reformers', outside a Church where the Reformation was first preached. The Queen thought the Service resembled that of the Scottish Church, except that the singing of the chorales by the whole congregation was an experience quite unique. It was not only the Lutheran Service which put the Queen in mind of Scotland. The Thuringian landscape, with the hills piling up towards Gotha, reminded her strongly of Perthshire and Aberdeenshire. The peasants were welcoming and dutiful, the men, with fur caps doffed, picturesque in coloured jackets with steel buttons, breeches and stockings, the women and children in gay dresses. They were, remarked the Queen, quite poor, but also quite clean; 'and this is because they are peasants, and do not aspire to be more.'

Two days later the Prince celebrated his birthday.

To celebrate this dear day in my beloved husband's country and birthplace is more than I ever hoped for, and I am so thankful for it...I wished him joy so warmly, when the singers sang, as they did the other morning. Then the band played, and beautifully, a Chorale and Reveil, and several other pretty things; amongst others, the March and 'O Isis and Osiris!' from the *Zauberflöte*....The day was the finest and warmest and brightest summer day imaginable, which is of good omen to dearest Albert. Later in the day, some of the peasants came up in gala dress, two and two, preceded by music; the women many of them with wreaths on their heads, and the men's hats decorated with ribbons and flowers. The first couple came up to us, and the woman presented a wreath to my dearest Albert, and the man a nosegay to me, saying at the same time, in German 'I congratulate you on your husband's birthday, and wish that he may live for many and many a year, and that you may soon come back!' They danced, shouting (*jauchzend*) in that peculiar way they have here.

They waltzed and danced the polka extremely well.

When they left Coburg, the Queen and the Prince went to Meiningen, where the reigning Duke was a relative by marriage. From Meiningen they went to Schmalkalden and then up to Gotha. As in ancient times nobility had been welcomed in Thuringia with specially written cantatas of welcome so now Philipp Welcker's *Thüringens Grüsse*...was performed.

*Preist die Herrin der Meere,*

chorussed the land-locked choristers of Gotha as the cantata approached its climax, which was reached with:

*Als Albion auf des Himmels Wort*
*Den Meer enstieg, des Lichtes froh,*
*Da ward diess Vorrecht ihm hinfort*
*Und schützend sangen Engel so:*
    *Roll' Britannia, Britannia, roll' die Flut!*
    *Freiheit sey dein ew'ges Gut!*

The librettist apologised for the translation, but pointed out that there were those in Gotha who did not understand the English original. From Gotha Victoria and Albert paid a pious visit to the Wartburg and paid their respects to the citizens of Eisenach in memory of him who was, it was claimed, 'the beginning and the end of all music'.

Back in England, however, feelings of anti-monarchists and of anti-Albertians were agitated by other events during this Germany excursion. *Punch* let loose a fusillade against the monarchy and against blood-sports. Two cartoons contrasted the 'Court Pastimes' of the Elizabethans and the Victorians to the disadvantage of the latter. An unnamed poet, but probably Thackeray, lambasted the Prince for his part in the stag hunt at Gotha that was let into the programme; while *Punch* also quoted a letter from an eye-witness previously published in the *Standard*. '[The deer-killing] was very shocking. The Queen wept. *I saw large tears in her eyes*: and Her Majesty tells me that she with difficulty kept the chair during what followed. When the Queen saw the otter hunt in Scotland the pity that she *naturally felt* at the death of the animal was *counterbalanced by a knowledge of his propensities*, so that it is almost as meritorious to *destroy an otter as it is a snake*; but this was a totally different case; nor is Her Majesty yet recovered. *For the Prince*, the deer were too numerous, and *must* be killed. *This* was the German method; and no doubt the reigning Duke will distribute them to his people, who will thank Prince Albert for providing them venison'.

Sir George meanwhile had returned to England, having added to his already recorded memories some which complemented the experiences of the royal family. A loyal subject, and an officer of the Court, Sir George did not fail from time to time to think reverently about his monarch.

Friday, August 15
Got up early to finish my packing, which I did before Breakfast, a wet Morning: it must have rained hard during the Night, but it was Moonlight when I went to bed. This day being the Assumption (a great day in R. Catholic Countries) about ½ past 7 this Morning a queer sort of a Procession came into the Market Place and stopped just below our Hotel, when they seemed to say a Prayer and then moved on, there was only one Priest and some men with dirty Flags

and other men with Staves. There were 2 lighted Candels. They sung
nearly all the time in Unison, not effective, the whole was a shabby
affair, they seemed to be Countrymen (about 100) in Blue frocks who
formed the Procession. When it arrived among the Women (who
were in the Market about 6 every Morning with their Baskets) most
of them seemed to join it, going first before the Priest. All the men
had their hats off.

After Breakfast went to buy some Views at a Bookseller's near our
Hotel, from thence called on Liszt, at the Golden Star. He went to
Coblentz yesterday. Next we all 3 went to call upon Mr and Mrs
Hodgson at the Belle Vue Hotel. They went yesterday. The Rain was
so disagreeable that we returned home thro' the Minster Platz which
was full of Booths for the Fair, a Dutch Clock stuck up at the Church
Door. A ragged old woman said something to us which I took for
abuse, another Woman standing by said she was paying us a
*compliment*. Robertson did not understand her.

Mr Robertson and his Nephew left our Hotel 1/4 before 12 in the
Omnibus to go by the Steam Boat to Coblentz, intending to sleep
there if they can obtain Beds. Our Press Gang went there for the gay
doings & Fetes to our Queen, who is staying with the King of P. at
his Castle Stolzenfels near Coblentz. Tomorrow the Robertsons intend
to go from thence per Steam in one day to Mannheim.

At – 12 – o'Clock Noon I left our Hotel in our Omnibus (that is I
was to have gone in the Omnibus which today would be the first
time – *it was too late*, therefore Simrock desired me *to walk* as fast as I
could, which I did in the Rain most uncomfortably, with the Boots
carrying my Bag and got there before Mr Boots, and just got my
Bag weighed and took out my Ticket about 2 Minutes before the
Train started. I offered Boots 3 or 4 Groscen [*sic*] but he pointed to a
Silver Piece in my hand wishing me to give him that, jabbering that
I had not offered him enough, but I was not to be done, therefore as
I had no time to look for a small Piece, as the Train was just going
off he got nothing) for the Railway Station. The Train left for
Cologne at 10 m past 1.

I was advised to go in the 2 Class which I found very nearly as
comfortable as the first – excellent Windows and soft seats but covered

with Black Leather. They did not give me any Ticket for my Luggage but I had no difficulty in getting it at Cologne. There were only 3 of us in the Carriage, both the others smoked, which is not allowed in *some* of the 2nd Class Carriages, & Robertson said it is so written on those Carriages but I had not time to study the outsides being in such a hurry to get in.

I had a good view of the palace of Brühl, where our Queen first arrived on her visit to the King of Prussia, it does not seem a large Palace, it is certainly too close to the Railway. It is rather nearer to Cologne than to Bonn. A Porter at the Station [in Cologne] took my Bag to a Vigilant or Fiacre (Cab with one horse). I thought I was to have it to myself but I found a Gent in it who did not speak much French, however we came direct to the Hotel de Vienne, the same we were in on our way to Bonn, the Gent went further. I was in time for the Table d'Hote. Had a good dinner but annoyed with the music from 2 Italians, Harp and Guitar, one of them sung badly 'Largo al factotum' and with bad taste for this country, 'Allons enfans'. I gave the Woman who collected about 4 Pfennig. I sat next a Gent who had come from Aix la Chapelle to see the Sights and was to return by Train this Evening at 6 – he said there had been many Robberies in Cologne but some of the Thieves had been taken, they came from Belgium.

After Dinner in a soaking Rain I made out my way to the Ostend Railway Station with the aid of the Map and asking occasionally. I went a great part of the way by the Rhine and returned a different way, passing through strong Fortifications into the town. The Railway Station is outside the Gates (so is the Bonn R.S.). I would not have gone in the heavy rain but I wished to make sure about the Railway tomorrow morning. I was much disappointed in being told by the Money-taker at the Bureau that I could only pay as far as Aix-la-Chapelle. I am now in a fuss as to whether my *Bag* is to be directed to this place or Ostend. To save trouble and to prevent my leaving the *Blue* Bag in a Carriage, as I had nearly done in coming, I put everything into my large Bag, it would still hold more.

In going I went into the beautiful Cathedral. Prayers were being chanted, and the Organ (sounds well) just as I was coming out. I stopp'd of course but the singing was in Unison; it was like a Chant, between the verses, but Symphonies, occasionally. They say our Queen was at the ceremony of laying the first stone of a Tower but did not assist at it. I observed several Poles – where I suppose Flags had been hoisted (in the large Sq. near the Cathedral) during the Queen's visit to this large City – no *side* Pavements but better paved than at Bonn.

In coming back to the Hotel I had nearly got into a scrape. I met a similar Procession to the one I saw at Bonn this morning, at least 500 Persons walking, and what I suppose *they* called singing. They were in 2 Rows – the Women came first. Rather old and ugley [*sic*], few young ones among them. Next the Men, in the same sort of Blue frocks as at Bonn. I observed they had no hats on, but most of them, Men and Women, had Umbrellas. I stood looking indeed waiting to go bye in a narrow St not liking to cross the Procession, when first one man and then another, not in the Procession, but seemed to come out of a Public House, came up and seemed very angry, not one word could I understand, but I luckily guest that I ought to be uncovered, off went my hat and away they went but looked very cross. There I stood until they were all gone.

I found out the Hotel with only asking once, wet through, there-fore changed directly and had my shoes dried and cleaned. It is very cold in the Coffee Room, a Fire would be a luxury which I hope they are enjoying at Hythe. This seems a fine town but the Rain pre-vented my seeing it to advantage.

Went to bed in a good room early; the noise in and out of the Hotel (for it is near the Poste Royale) was so great that I could not sleep until 12 o'Clock. Soon after I had to make a visit (curious place, a hole to look in at the side to see if it was occupied.) The Waiter promised to bring the Bill tonight in my Room, he did not, and I had the greatest difficulty to get it in time in the Morning. The waiter seem'd worn out with fatigue.

f.78

Expenses
After my Settlement with Mr Robertson

August 15 Friday
Bought View of Gand
    ditto     Bruges
    ditto     Malines
    ditto     Bonn
They cost 24 Sil: Gros: or 3 Francs each
they 4 cost in English money 9$^8$7$^d$

f.77v

Expenses from Bonn to Ostend
August 15 Friday:
left Hotel for Railway to Cologne at 12
Train went at 10 past 12 Noon
Arrived at Cologne at 10 past 1

| | F. | G. |
|---|---|---|
| Had to walk instead of an Omnibus from Hotel to Station | | |
| 2nd Class to Cologne from Bonn | | 10 |
| Luggage | | 1 |
| Vigilant from the Station to Hotel de Vienne – one Gent came in it also } | | 5 |
| August 16 Saturday | | |
| Bill at Hotel de Vienne very civil & attentive Waiter the *last time* we were there, but not attentive this time. | | 5 |
| About 7 Franc | | 2½ |

August 16th, Saturday.
After a good dish of Coffee and Rolls, one of which I put in my
Pocket, the Omnibus called at the Hotel about ½ past 5 Morng. and
took me and 2 other Gents in the Hotel to the Station I walk'd to
last night. The same Person I then spoke to yesterday afternoon,
made not the slightest difficulty in taking the amount all the way
from here to Ostend, very little difficulty in having my Bag weighed.
There were not many Passengers from hence. Left Cologne at 15 m.
past 6 Morng. Changed Carriages at Verviers, the 1st Station from
Cologne on the Belgium [*sic*] Frontier (but had a Sandwich previous at
Aix la Chapelle Station at 9 in the Morng.) We had to stop more

than an hour at Verviers while the Luggage was examined; *all of it* was taken out of the Waggons which *brought* it, into the other that took it to Ostend, a most tiresome affair. The Luggage was put into a kind of Shed, on a sort of long Square deal Table. As each Box etc. was brought in the owner had to find it, when it came into the Shed, and then was asked if he had anything to declare and to open his Trunk. Mine was but slightly examined, I saw some others searched more attentively but on the whole they examined the small parcels but not inclined to untie the Cords on the large Boxes. The search should be strict or not at all for it gives much trouble to all parties. When I had lock'd my bag I lugged it out of the Shed, and gave it to the man who was loading the Baggage. How things are so accurately delivered at the different Stations is astonished [*sic*] considering the enormous quantity. When the luggage is weighed a Number is pasted generally *over* the direction on the Box, a similar Number is given to you when you pay according to Weight. On the Ticket you receive and on that pasted on the luggage is the place where you paid for it, and the place where you are to claim it and to deliver up the Ticket to a man who examines if the number you give corresponds with that on the Box. A most troublesome affair both to have it weighed and the push to reclaim it.

In the Carriage from Cologne was an intelligent Gent and his Son who had just come from the Cape of Good Hope. Upon getting into the Carriage from Verviers I found Mr Saust, who seemed travelling with a Gent and his Wife; he had come from Aix la Chapelle and was going from Malines to Brussels. We changed Carriages again at Malines and had by comparison an uncomfortable one, a Gent said was one of the first, it had no division and the seats are not with Air Cushions. Malines is a curious and large Station (see View) 4 or 5 Trains all at the same time at the Station, therefore it was most difficult to get into the right one, and to add to the confusion a Regiment of Soldiers (but without Arms) came with us from Malines to Ghent, they then went in the Lille train. They were amusing themselves with jumping off the Train at every Station and singing badly. Thank God we arrived safely at Ostend about 1/4 or 20 m past 9 Eveng. My bag came out nearly the last, I then carried it to the Gate where I gave up my Ticket. A Porter took it to the Omnibus in waiting for the Hotel l'Allemande (recommended by Lady Westmoreland) where they were so full that I could only have a Bed Room on the second floor, which was good; the Sheets were almost the best I have slept in any where. I had a Veal Cutlet and some Potatoes not particularly well dressed & a Glass of Brandy to kill the bad Water here which Murray truly mentions. I went to my room about ½ past 11, it is very fatiguing to come from Cologne to Ostend in one day about [lacuna] miles upwards of 15 hours journey. I think it could be done under 12 hours if there were not the stops for searching the Baggage (during which you must take care that a Trunk is not thrown upon you) and at Malines and other Stations, *when going* it is fast enough but not then so fast as in England.

The Persons I travelled with from Malines were all foreigners, one Gent from Aix la Chapelle said the Waters had done his Rheumatism no good; I saw many Englishmen in the Train, but no one that I knew, except Saust and he is a Dutchman he said. Murray describes the Route so accurately that a Journalist is saved much Trouble. My Passport was not asked for *at any Town* on my return from Bonn to Dover.

## f.77

Aug. 16 Railway from Cologne to Ostend
N.B. I gave a Sovereign & 5 F. Pieces, he
returned me 2 F.
Luggage all the Way Paid at Cologne 14 Gros.
They gave me two Tickets at Cologne – one to
Herbesthal – 76 Gros. the other from
Herbesthal to Ostend – 17 F. 50 [C.?] or 4 Fr. 20 C.
Roll & Veal at Aix la Chapelle
at 9 in the Morng. 2 Gros.
Soup at Verviers, where the luggage was
examined – a Demi-Franc.
Sunday, August 18 [17 is meant]
Got up early not kept waiting long for Coffee or the Account. I do not think this Hotel comes up to Lady Westmoreland's recommendation, however, they said they were full. Mine was a good Bed Room

(2 Beds in it), though up 2 pair of Stairs. Part of it was so warm that
I was rather frightened until I made out that the hot wall might arise
from a Chimney being there.

A Porter carried my Bag from the Hotel to the Steam Boat 'The
Princess Alice', Capt. Smithers, the one we came from Dover in.
He remembered me again and said the Queen had a rough passage
last Sunday. We walked from the Hotel to the Vessel, fortunately it
did not rain *the whole day*. Last night they said the vessel would go
at 8 – I knew better for it does not depart till after the Train is in
from Ghent about 8 o'Clock every morning. The Bags went on board
about 1/4 to 9, for want of Water we could not get out of the
Harbour, but we left Ostend at about 1/4 past 9 – very rough indeed
crossing the Bar of the Harbour, where the Ondine shipped a heavy
sea in going out of the Harbour and would have been lost if any of
her machinery broke, which it did last week with many passengers
on board, who were landed at Margate etc. Fortunately one of the
Government Packets towed the Ondine in (for which they charged
her owners 75 guineas) or she would have been lost. Strong wind and
tide against us, many sick especially among the Ladies; soon after we
left Ostend they were lying on the Deck in the *best form* they could.
I was very queer for half the Voyage, but recovered towards the end
of it. 76 Passengers on board and some of them very agreeable,
particularly a Gent who had lived abroad for many years, described
Bonoparte's burial place after his body had been removed to France.
Another Gent informed me that he had been to Prague, Vienna and
Hungary to make out his Pedigree and had confirmed to his own
satisfaction, that he is by descent related to most of the crowned
heads of Europe, among them, tho' distantly, to our Queen (thro'
Prince Leiningen, the Duc. of Kent's 1st Husband) thereby he hoped
the Queen would give his son a Deanery! or something of the sort.
It appeared to me that he was a little cracked about his Pedigree;
it had cost him upwards of £1000 and he would have to pay a great
deal more. Seeing my name in my hat he claimed acquaintance
immediately, said I had once chosen a P. forte for his Sister and told
me his name was *Wrattislaw*, that he knew the Fullers well, that they
were out of town but he should knock up the Servants to obtain a

bed. Mr Fuller's Partner was a relation of this Mr Wrattislaw he said.

Captn. Heaviside, whose wife ran away with Dr Lardner, was on board. This Captn. is a very tall man. It seems that whether there be many or few Passengers in the Steam Vessels it makes no difference to the Captn. he being on a fixed Salary, all the Receipts going to the Government who pay all the Expences. We carry the mails to & from *Ostend*, the French carry *their* mails from Calais to England, our government of course take ours over.

Upon a Gent asking the Steward if he could purchase any eatables on board, he replied, 'Oh, yes! but you will not want them.' A pleasant allusion to the probability of sea-sickness. We began to recover our looks as we got near Dover; we arrived there about 1/4 to 3 being a 6½ Voyage. Though it blew hard, till we came under the English land, and the Tide against us. Fortunately it did not rain, being the 1st day without it for some days since.

Not water enough to go into the Harbour therefore we landed in Boats in the Bay were [sic] the Bathing Machines are, near the York Hotel. Nothing can be more disagreeable than landing in these boats. I suppose there is no real danger, unless the Sea is very rough, but by the people all rising together in the boat when alongside the Vessel, or in landing, tho' by the rocking of the Boat they may stumble, as I did and scraped my Shin Bone very much. In landing the waves beat the boat against the Beach. With the assistance of a Sailor I jumped out and escaped the Waves, but several of the Passengers got very wet, one Lady had to dry herself by the fire. A Gent *bought* a pair of Stockings (tho' on a Sunday, he said to the vendor he must sell them as a work of Charity to save his catching a Cold) for all the Baggage was taken to the Custom House. It was landed in Boats very soon after us and placed on the Beach, when from thence taken by Hand Carts to the C. House near the *Ship Hotel*, I called twice. Expected to find a letter from Margaret about Omnibus from Folkstone – no letter – she had written to Bonn expecting that I should receive it on Friday Morning last. Went to the Custom House and had to wait in a Room. The passengers who came by the *French* mail were 1st called to claim *their* luggage – none answered – Next the Passengers from Ostend were called, those who had but *one* Single Packet were called first, about 6 or 8 at a time were admitted. This seems a good regulation. I went in with the 2nd Batch. The moment my name was mentioned the Head Clerk took off his hat and said, of course you have come from Bonn, was most exceedingly Polite. We chatted about the Festival while a man very slightly examined my one Bag, which I was previously desired to point out in the room among a long Row of Carpet Bags. My examination finished, my Bag was put out of a hole at the bottom of a door and I was desired to walk out of a door close to the hole; a Porter took my bag from the Custom House to the R.way Station for which he said I had Sixpence to pay. Had he left the remuneration to me he would have had a shilling. A R.way Porter civilly let me into the 1st Class Waiting Room where I doctored my leg with some of Dr. Billing's plaster which I took with me to Germany with Pills and Powders supplied by Margaret.

Left Dover by Train this Sunday evening at half past 6. They put me into the Couppée where the Surveyor of the Packet Boats of the Folkstone Harbour came with me to Folkstone. It was well that he did for I most carelessly left my Umbrella in the couppée. The advantage of having my name on it caused me to get it again, thus – as no Omnibus goes from the Folkstone Station to Hythe on a Sunday night. I hir'd a Fly and had just got into Folkstone when the Driver of another fly came quickly afterwards bringing my Umbrella for which he said he *claimed* 6d, because he had come so fast. I should have given him a 1ˢ had he not fixed the sum – we came a very good pace from Folkstone to Hythe where I arriv'd safe & well thanks be to God – and found all well at Mrs Love's – got there about 8 in the Evening.

On Sept 14 1845 – I returned to Mr J. Ries (when he called at my House) *all* the Railroad Papers & a Book he lent me, and I gave him the Printed Copy of his Father's Diploma as a Dr.

f. 76v

August 17th
Bill at Hotel d'Allemande, Ostende for Bed, Supper & Breakfast and for the Omnibuss [*sic*] to the Hotel from the Railway Station –

7 Francs all but a 1/4 of a Frank, which they gave me in Change.

| | £ | s | d |
|---|---|---|---|
| Commission for taking my Bag to Steam Boat (one Franc) | | | 10 |
| Paid for Passage in Steam Boat to Dover | 1 | 1 | 0 |
| Steward | | 1 | 0 |
| Porter taking Bag from the Custom House to R.W.Station | | | 6 |
| R.way 1st Class to Folk stone | | 1 | 6 |
| Omnibus man bringing my Umbrella which I left in R:way Carriage at Folk stone | | | 6 |
| Fly from Folkstone to Hythe | | 5 | 0 |
| Driver | | 1 | 0 |

There follows this summary, which begins on f.75v (7 being blank)

1845

| | £ | s | d |
|---|---|---|---|
| Took to Bonn £35 0 0 money | | | |
| Brought from | | | |
| Notes | 15 | | |
| Sovereigns | 3 | 10 | 0 |
| Silver & Copper | | 9 | 4 |
| | 18 | 19 | 4 |
| 2½ Francs (French) in English Money | | 2 | 1 |
| | 19 | 1 | 5 |
| Took | 35 | | |
| Brought Home | 19 | 1 | 5 |
| Expences from August 4th to 17th | 15 | 18 | 7 |
| Previous Expences in going to Dover etc. | 1 | 4 | 3 |
| Murray's Book bought of Messrs Calkin & Budd | | 10 | 6 |
| Prussian Money bought of Mr J. Ries – which I spent at Bonn, except for a few Coins which I gave to Rose on my return | | 7 | 2 |
| Total Expences | 18 | 0 | 6 |

f.75

*Bills*

No 1 Ship Hotel – Dover August 5th

No 2 Hotel Lion d'Or                5th

No 3 'Hotel de Vienne' Cologne 6th

No 4 'Wein Karte' st Nonnenworth 11th

No 5 Dinner at '*Goldenen* (sic) Stern' 13th

No 6 Bill from Simrock

'Hôtel de Treves' Bonn

  from August 7th to 15th

No 7 'Hotel de Vienne' Cologne 15th

No 8 'Hotel d'Allemagne' Ostend 17th

# CHAPTER 12

# Finale

Smart had decided to go at least into partial retirement before he went to Germany in 1845. He was, after all, nearly seventy and although he had weathered the tempests of time better than most he was inclined to leave more gaps for leisure in the daily timetable than there had been formerly. He first of all determined that he would no more conduct in London. He was reluctant, however, to cut himself off entirely from the public life and he directed occasional concerts for some years to come. His last appearance was on 27 April 1852, at the opening of the Town Hall, Chertsey. Even after that he continued to superintend the private entertainments of some of the nobility.

Smart had been a professor at the Royal Academy of Music since its foundation. He gave up this appointment in 1850, but his zeal for teaching and his interest in his pupils remained lively. Among those who came to him for advice and instruction in his later years were Jenny Lind (after her American tour of 1850 far and away the greatest singer in the world) and Henriette Sontag, both of whom were convinced that where interpretation of Handel was concerned Sir George was the final authority. When the question of a memorial to Mendelssohn was under consideration and a London committee was established to inaugurate a Mendelssohn Scholarship, Smart naturally emerged as its Chairman. It gratified him in due course to notice the spectacular progress of the first holder of this Scholarship.

Arthur Sullivan owed his place as a chorister in the Chapel Royal to Smart, who had instructed Helmore, the Master of the Choristers, that he should be admitted. Smart went out of his way to encourage the young Sullivan and to arrange for his first anthems to be sung in the Chapel Royal. He watched Sullivan's career at the Royal Academy and was delighted when Potter wrote to him approving the boy's industry and growing skills.[1] Sullivan went to Leipzig and Moscheles kept Sir George informed of his progress. When it seemed, despite the Leipzig professors' opinion that he should extend his studies there, that Sullivan would have to come home through there being no funds available, Smart promptly helped him with a personal contribution. On completing his studies Sullivan wrote a thank-you letter to Smart. When, three years later, he learned of Smart's death he wrote a heart-felt note of condolence to Lady Smart.[2]

Smart retained his post as Organist of the Chapel Royal until the end of his life, and his memoranda on the arrangements for the special occasions that proliferated in the middle years of the Victorian era show that his eye for detail remained undimmed. Smart becomes something of a historic figure in his own right as we envisage him attending to his more ceremonial Chapel duties in the Blue Queen's Coat, White Waistcoat, Black Pantaloons, Shining Boots, White Gloves, and Folding Hat (for ornament and not for use) that had been proper to his office for centuries. The only refinement he allowed himself on a January day in 1858 for a royal wedding was an 'extra, sleeveless, flannel waistcoat', even so the Chapel was warm and he did not need to wear it. The wedding that took place that day was between the Princess Victoria, Princess Royal, and Crown Prince Friedrich Wilhelm of Prussia, from which union came the last of the German Emperors.

Smart lived in an age of revolution, both industrial and otherwise. In 1825 he had gone from Leipzig to Berlin and Potsdam by the same coach route as J. S. Bach had travelled only 80 years earlier. In 1845 he had had to accustom himself to the excitements and tribulations of conveyance by rail. In youth he had played on the kind of organ that had satisfied Handel. In the 1830's and 40's he was still trying to come to terms with the new-fangled pedal-board while admiring the prodigious advances in technological skill made by such builders as William Hill and Gray & Davison.

1. In a letter, dated 17 July 1857; Add.Ms.41771, f.133.
2. See Percy M. Young, *Sir Arthur Sullivan*, London, 1971, p.277.

The scientific spirit of the age was expressed through the Great Exhibition in Hyde Park, in 1851. Smart was up with all that was going on and on 1 May found himself nominally in command of the Great Organ and the five other organs dispersed round the building and their organists, the Royal Choirs, the choruses of the Royal Academy and the Sacred Harmonic Society, two military bands, the full team of State Trumpeters, and all the most eminent orchestral players and singers in London. Smart had been an indispensable part of great socio-musical occasions for half-a-century. Throughout that period – as from time immemorial – the musicians had been expected to 'give their services'.

In 1857 he 'gave in addition to C. F. Smart's' subscription of 1/- to 'Handel's Statue at Halle 4/-'. On 4 February 1858, he sent £5 on his account 'thro' Mr Rose' to the Handel Committee. So far as Smart was concerned, Handel was the beginning and the end of musical wisdom. As a boy Smart had grown up under the influence of those who had known Handel – his master Arnold had been a pupil of Handel's friend Bernard Gates and also a Chapel Royal chorister during the period in which the most of the oratorios had been composed. Smart maintained the Handel connection with the Royal Family. Parts of the Funeral Anthem that Handel had written for Queen Caroline in 1737 were still being sung under Smart's direction at royal obsequies a hundred years later! For more cheerful occasions at Court the 'Hallelujah' Chorus from *Messiah* was obligatory – although after 1815 Smart also supplied the corresponding chorus from Beethoven's *Mount of Olives*.

Smart's interests stretched back to the madrigalists and at a time when the general taste was for glees that were less demanding on the ear and the musical sense he put pieces by Morley and Wilbye into concerts at the Mansion House or at St James's, and Kensington Palaces. In old age he supported George Macfarren and William Chappell in their musicological enterprises. For the Handel Society he edited the 'Dettingen' *Te Deum*, for the Musical Antiquarian Society a volume of Orlando Gibbons's first set of madrigals.

A century after his death Smart's credentials may look a little dusty. He has, however, a claim on our gratitude, for, more than any other person, he made music available for the many. He walked with Kings but had the common touch. He was at ease at Court, but he understood the ways and appreciated the talents of the working class choral singers of Lancashire and Yorkshire. It was largely through him that Handel's music became a social force in industrial England and Wales. It was Smart who conducted the first performance of Haydn's *The Creation* in England. He made himself personally responsible for the production of Spohr's *Azor and Zemira* at Covent Garden, while he introduced that composer's *Last Judgement* at a Norwich Festival. He helped to open the eyes of the English to the felicities of the music of Mendelssohn and to make the name of Beethoven a household word. When Weber died Smart was quick to propose that a suitable memorial should be raised to his memory. Although Weber's body was removed from London without any notification being given to any of his English friends (a fact which piqued Smart considerably) the initiative for the erection of a memorial in Dresden came from London. A notice was circulated stating that 'A monument to the memory of this illustrious composer is about to be erected at Dresden, similar in design and magnificence to that which has been lately erected to Beethoven, at Bonn...' Smart and Julius Benedict collected subscriptions and sent them to Dresden through Hebeler, who was still the Prussian Consul in London.

It was only three years later that Smart heard that the money had reached Dresden, when he had a receipt from Weber's widow. And more years were to elapse before the monument was built. On 28 November 1861, Smart wrote to Weber's son. He was more than a little hurt. Even now, aged 85, he would have gone again to Dresden:

> Among the Papers you will receive there is one allusion to the £30 I sent to Dresden being Subscriptions *in England* towards the Monument to the late C.M. von Weber. I understand this Monument has been erected at Dresden, *but no information* of it has been given to me. This I much regret, as I have not been enabled to make any *official* communication to the Subscribers; – I was honored with an invitation (being a Subscriber) to the Inauguration of the Monument to Beethoven at Bonn in 1845 – at which I was present; from the great esteem and regard I have to the memory of your Father, and in consideration of his last days having been passed in my house, I should have been much gratified by an invitation to have joined in the

just tribute to his worth and talents. I shall be much obliged by you giving me a description of this monument and of the ceremony at the Inauguration of it.

Smart had a great delight in living. He carefully noted the details of refreshment offered to the musicians on State and civic occasions, but did not always show himself as uncritical of the quality of food and drink. He was a consistent party-goer, yet he loved the domesticities provided by Lady Smart. He was devoted to his daughter Margaret Rose (b. 1837), and it was with special pleasure that he conducted wife and daughter round St James's Palace in 1858 to show them the preparations for the Royal Wedding.

He was generous. In youth he had paid his father's debts and given assistance to members of his family, as also to his apprentices. The list of his benefactions was a long one, and the needs of the young he was never able to resist. On 2 June 1852, he was approached by a deputation of sportsmen. His response stands in his memorandum book: 'West. Abbey Boys for Cricket Match 2/6'.

In 1864 a College of Organists was founded. At the inaugural dinner the Chairman was Sir George Smart who

. . . offered some valuable advice and pointed out the many difficulties which usually beset the path of organists, who, as a body, were a material part of the Churches, although he feared that, unhappily, neither their efforts nor themselves were sufficiently appreciated. . .[3]

Three years later Sir George died. It was typical of him that on his deathbed he was making orderly arrangements for his own funeral. With his death both the baroque and classical eras of English music came to an end. And so –

We are again reminded of the comparative youth of what is termed modern music, by the fact of Sir George Smart having lived in the days of Haydn, Mozart, and Beethoven; and as a link between his own time and that of Handel, it is a curious fact that he had often heard from Joah Bates (who, as a boy, had seen Handel direct his oratorios), many circumstances connected with the precise manner in which Handel's greatest works were

3. P. A. Scholes, *The Mirror of Music*, London, 1947, II, p. 609.

first performed in the country; so that even as an authority upon this subject, his information was highly valuable. To the honourable conduct, strict integrity, and singleness of purpose which characterised the long professional life of Sir George Smart, every one who knew him, either publicly or privately, will bear ample testimony. As we have before said, he has stamped his name upon the history of music in England...[4]

4. *The Musical Times*, xiii, 1 April 1867, p. 35.

# Appendix

The relative values of French and Belgian, English, and Prussian currencies in 1845, as noted by Smart in his diary.

| *French currency* | | £ | s | d |
|---|---|---|---|---|
| 1 gold Napoleon or Louis | 20 Francs | 16 | 8 | |
| 1 silver piece | 5 | | 4 | 2 |
| ,, ,, | 3 | | 2 | 6 |
| ,, ,, | 2 | | 1 | 8 |
| ,, ,, | 1 | | | 10 |
| ,, ,, | Demi-franc | | | 5 |
| 1 copper piece | Double sous (10 centimes) | | | 1 |
| | Sous (5 centimes) | | | $\frac{1}{2}$ |

A sovereign now is equal at par in French money to 24 Francs

| *Prussian money* | | | | |
|---|---|---|---|---|
| 1 [silver] Thaler | | | 3 | |
| 1 silver piece | 10 Groschen | | 1 | |
| ,, ,, | 5 | | | 6 |
| ,, ,, | $2\frac{1}{2}$ | | | 3 |
| ,, ,, | 1 (= 12 copper Pfennige) | | | 1 |
| ,, ,, | $\frac{1}{2}$ (= 6 ,, ,, ) | | | $\frac{1}{2}$ |
| 1 copper piece | 3 Pfennige | | | $\frac{1}{4}$ |

£1 English is equal to 6 Thalers & 20 Silver Groschen. The value varies according to the Exchange.

Smart went into the subject in even more detail, and took the trouble to sketch the designs of certain coins in order the more easily to recognise them when abroad.

# Bibliography

C. BACHE (translator), *Letters of Franz Liszt*. London, 1894

A. C. BENSON and (W.L. Brett) VISCOUNT ESHER, *The Letters of Queen Victoria*. London 1907

H. K. BREIDENSTEIN, *Festgabe zu der am 12ten August 1845 stattfindenden Inauguration des Beethoven-Monuments*. Bonn, 1845

H. K. BREIDENSTEIN, *Zur Jahresfeier der Inauguration des Beethoven-Monuments*. Bonn, 1846

H. B. COX and C. L. E. COX (ed.), *Leaves from the Journal of Sir George Smart*. London, 1907

THEODOR FRIMMEL, *Beethoven-Handbuch*, 2 vol. Leipzig, 1926

H. J. GAUNTLETT, 'Beethoven and the Philharmonic Society', in *The Musical World*, 5, no. 59, p.97. London, 1837

R. B. GOTCH (ed.) *Mendelssohn and his friends in Kensington* (*Letters from Fanny and Sophy Horsley*). London, 1934

S. HENSEL (ed.) *The Mendelssohn family*, 2 vol. London, 1881

G. HOGARTH, *The Philharmonic Society of London*. London, 1862

C. MACLEAN, 'Sir George Smart, Musician-Diarist', in *Sammelbände der Internationalen Musikgesellschaft*, no.X, March 1909

T. MARTIN, *The Life of His Royal Highness the Prince Consort*, 5 vol. London, 1875

F. MOSCHELES, *Letters of Felix Mendelssohn to Ignaz and Felix Moscheles*. London, [1888]

D. OLLIVIER (ed.), *Correspondance de Liszt et de la Comtesse d'Agoult, 1883–64*, 2 vol. Paris, 1933–4

C. POTTER, 'Recollections of Beethoven, with Remarks on his Style', in *The Musical World*, 1, no7, p.101. London, 1836

J. RICHARDSON, *My dearest Uncle: A Life of Leopold I, First King of the Belgians*. London, 1961

A. F. SCHINDLER, *Beethoven as I knew him* (trans. C. S. Jolly, ed. D. W. MacArdle). London, 1966

P. A. SCHOLES, *The Mirror of Music 1844–1944*, 2 vol., London, 1947.

L. SPOHR, *Selbstbiographie*. Cassel/Göttingen, 1860–61
*Louis Spohr's Autobiography* (trans.) London, 1865

N. TEMPERLEY, 'Tempo and repeats in the early nineteenth century', in *Music and Letters*, 47, no.4, pp.323–336. London, Oct.1966

P. H. WELCKER, *Thüringens Grüsse bei der Ankunft Ihrer Majestät der Königin Victoria von Grossbritannien und Irland*. Gotha, 1845

P. J. WILLETTS, *Beethoven and England*: An Account of the Sources in the British Museum. London, 1970

J. WILSHERE, *William Gardiner of Leicester (1770–1853), Hosiery Manufacturer, Musician and Dilettante*. Leicester, 1970

*The Musical World*, 28 August – 9 October, 1845

*New Musical Fund Concert Programmes*, 1794 – (B.M., C.61.g.20)

*Philharmonic Society Programmes*, 1813 – (B.M., M.K. 6.d.3)

*A Practical Rhine Guide by an Englishman Abroad*. London/Leipzig, 1857

*Belgium and Nassau: or, The Continental Tourist*. London [1838]

*Bradshaw's Continental Railway, Steam Navigation, and Conveyance Guide and Traveller's Manual for the whole Continent of Europe*. Paris/London/Manchester, 1847

*Bradshaw's Illustrated Hand-book for travellers in Belgium, in the Rhine and through portion of Rhenish Prussia*. London, 1855

*New Handbook for the River Rhine from Cologne to Mayence*. Cologne, 1843

*Der Passagier im Königreich Belgien*. Berlin, 1845

*Der Rhein und die Rheinlände*. Darmstadt and Wiesbaden, 1846

*The Rhine, its scenery and its monuments, drawn from Nature by eminent artists*. London, 1862

# Index